-I Can -
CHOOSE
JOY
with God

OTHER BOOKS AND AUDIO PRODUCTS
BY GANEL-LYN CONDIE

I Can Do Hard Things with God

I Can Forgive with God

I Can Choose Joy with God

Mother to Mother

The Decision That Changed My Life

The Perfect Gift

You Are More Than Enough: You Are Magnificent

Find Your Happy

You Are Already Walking on Water

Lionproof

I Can ~

CHOOSE

JOY

with God

STORIES OF HOPE
FROM FAITHFUL WOMEN

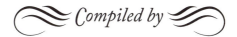 *Compiled by*

GANEL-LYN
CONDIE

with foreword by
CHAD HYMAS

Covenant Communications, Inc.

To my brothers and sisters on this side of the pond and on the other,
on this side of the veil and on the other,
I feel joy just thinking about you.

To my family
Thank you for believing that my time behind the computer and
speaking in the field are worthy efforts in ministering.

To my Covenant family
You make work more wonderful.

To my faith friends
You know who you are. Thank you for helping me out of the weeds
when I sometimes get lost and start wandering and wondering.

God expects you to have enough faith, determination, and trust in Him to keep moving, keep living, keep rejoicing. He expects you not simply to face the future; He expects you to embrace and shape the future—to love it, rejoice in it, and delight in your opportunities. God is eagerly waiting for the chance to answer your prayers and fulfill your dreams, just as He always has. But He can't if you don't pray, and He can't if you don't dream. In short, He can't if you don't believe.

—Jeffrey R. Holland[1]

---

1 Jeffrey R. Holland, "This, the Greatest of All Dispensations," *Ensign*, July 2007. Originally from a CES fireside address given on September 12, 2004.

Contents

Part V: Mission

Foreword
By Chad Hymas

IN THIS BEAUTIFUL COLLECTION OF testimonials, Ganel-Lyn Condie captures the very essence of what "joy" is in the eyes of our Father in Heaven. Joy is not a perfect life. It is not money. It is not perfect health, nor is it a collection of worldly assets. In this accumulation of masterfully documented accounts, you will find a commonality: "men are, that they might have joy,"[2] and joy is the pure love of Christ! And those who find it are seeking the treasures of God, not the treasures of the world, despite having adversity and going through major tragedies. In fact, one of the commonalities we see in the world is that the most joyful people are those who have fewer worldly possessions to their name. I wonder why that is? Heavenly Father gives to us when the world takes away. Tragically, it took my broken back for me to find God's true joy in this life.

Joy. How do we find it? More importantly, how do we find joy amidst adversity?

I thought I knew what joy was, how to find it, and how to live it. Life was moving along smoothly. I had two wonderful kids and an incredible wife. Life was good for our young family. We were happy. It looked like smooth sailing from here to the horizon, but it was just the calm before the storm.

At the age of twenty-seven, on the evening of April 3, 2001, my life and my family's changed forever. I was on my way home from work when Shondell called to tell me our youngest son had just taken his first steps. I told her I would hurry, but first, I needed to stop by the field to feed the elk.

I jumped onto the tractor and slid the steel forks under a one-ton bale of hay at the top of the pile. As I manipulated the controls to lift the monster bale clear, the hydraulic hoses spasmed. The forks holding the bale failed, and the bale fell back onto the stack.

---

2 2 Nephi 2:25.

It was low on hydraulic fluid. I knew it, and besides, it was pretty obvious. It was a simple fix, remedied in six or seven minutes. I just had to go to the shed, grab a can of fluid, and fill the hydraulic reservoir. Then it would be done and ready to go. Safe and smart. But that would take too long. I wanted to see my one-year-old take his first steps.

Try again. I yanked the lever. This time, the hydraulic system jerked the forks upward. The huge bale broke free and rolled backward, falling toward me. The bale's crushing weight landed fully on me, slamming my face into the control panel, and my body went instantly numb and limp. I couldn't feel my feet, legs, hands—nothing. The only movement possible was a slight shrug of my shoulders.

I was paralyzed.

It took forty-eight minutes for Shondell to find me.

The first police officers on the scene couldn't move the hay—not a fraction of an inch. A thousand pounds each? Of course they couldn't move it.

"Cut the strings," I whispered. My voice was weak.

They couldn't hear me. Why didn't they cut the strings? They could have saved a long, tortured hour.

How heavy was hay? A piece of hay was about the weight of a feather. How many pieces of hay did it take to make two thousand pounds? Lots. That package of sixteen bazillion individual pieces of hay wrapped in a gigantic bundle was a crushing weight. But separated, it would have been nothing. There was a point to be made here, wasn't there? Was it too big?

Was it overwhelming?

Cut the strings—just cut the strings!

Are you buried under crushing burdens? Projects that are too huge? Schedules that are too complicated? Maybe you are trying to do too much at once—trying to do everything instead of doing something.

Cut the strings, and cut yourself free. Do one thing at a time—and get it done. Move "out of the strain of the doing, into the peace of the done."[3]

* * *

It was three o'clock on a particularly frustrating Wednesday afternoon at the hospital. Shondell and I were sitting on a mat, she steadying me with her hand on my leg—a hand I cannot feel. Frustrated and angry, I was struggling to put on a T-shirt.

---

3 Julia Louise Woodruff.

It was tough enough to have to relearn something a two-year-old could do, but to have my beautiful wife watch me struggle with my weakness, well, the frustration was overwhelming. Why had this happened to me? Why must I be helpless and miserable? Why . . . ?

The music stopped.

Everyone turned to the door. I twisted my body to look as well. There stood Elder Neal A. Maxwell, a General Authority for The Church of Jesus Christ of Latter-day Saints.

"Look! It's Elder Maxwell," I whispered to Shondell.

A visit by someone of Elder Maxwell's status was a great honor.

He paused in the doorway for a moment and looked about the room, connecting one by one with each individual. I don't know if you can imagine what it meant to someone struggling with life to be really looked at, to be really seen, but it meant everything to me.

Elder Maxwell's eyes rested on me, and he walked toward us. "You must be Chad Hymas. And this must be Shondell." He knew our names. He also knew the names of our children.

He knew where I served my mission and knew the details of my accident. This man had, in fact, come to see me—personally. He knelt on the mat beside us. The room grew very quiet. Regardless of anyone's particular religious beliefs, this man was well known and greatly respected in our community. He asked if he could give me a blessing.

Such blessings have special meaning and power. Given and received in faith, they bring comfort and healing to the sick. They also bring guidance to the lost and calm to the distressed. Still feeling angry and discouraged, I looked down and told him I didn't feel worthy of a blessing.

He assured me that I was. He asked Shondell to kneel on the floor in front of me and hold me steady. He placed his hands on my head and gave me a wonderful blessing of faith and hope. He also prayed for the other patients there. He prayed for the doctors, nurses, and therapists. He prayed for Shondell—that she would accept this bitter cup without resentment.

During our visit, Elder Maxwell revealed something very personal. He had leukemia. He had suffered from it for several years. He admitted that in the beginning, he asked God why he had to suffer this affliction. He had been called to travel throughout the world and serve God and didn't understand how he could fulfill his calling if he was sick.

He eventually learned through his own experience and prayerful contemplation that his leukemia and my paralysis and every other affliction and the challenges and problems they present are part of what help us appreciate and become more like the Savior. He believed with all his heart that struggles and challenges lead us to knowledge, growth, and joy—if we let them.

Elder Maxwell helped me realize I must look at my situation differently and gain something positive from it. His advice and his blessing helped me change my point of view and move in a new direction. I was bound and determined to find joy again.

In his book *The Impossible Just Takes a Little Longer*, Art Berg wrote, "Life changes. It is the nature of life to do so. For those in this life who choose not to change, life will change for you. And it is always more painful that way." Life changed for my family and me. However uncomfortable that change was, it was up to me to decide how to respond.

I initially reacted to my accident and especially to the resulting difficult circumstances with blame, then with regret. What should my response be now? I needed to ask the larger question: Did this happen for a purpose—or could I create a purpose for what had happened?

How could I turn the circumstances of the accident, even my loss of mobility, into an advantage? What could I do to have more joy? How could I respond to my paralysis and pain constructively rather than destructively? How could I use my experience of dealing with paralysis to enhance my ability to deal with other life challenges? Maybe I could use my experience to enhance life itself—the meaning of life—by helping others deal with their challenges.

Thoughts are powerful. A change in our thinking changes our lives. New thinking creates new assumptions. New assumptions create different feelings and attitudes. New attitudes create a new approach to old challenges. A new approach creates new circumstances.

Like anyone going through a traumatic ordeal, I had to make significant changes in order to survive and move forward. Most importantly, I had to change the way I thought. This was the only way to regain the joy I once had—that joy I so desperately longed for.

I Can Find Joy with God was compiled so that through the examples and stories of others, we can truly learn what it means to find joy. Joy comes from reading others' stories and truly feeling their experiences on their journey. Ganel-Lyn is a talented writer who shares stories that inspire the human soul to find joy with God. As you read through the stories of these individuals traveling on their own journeys, you will be touched to look deep inside yourself and find the true meaning of *finding joy with God*. Your thoughts and perceptions will begin to change. You will feel the Spirit and will be moved to become more joyful. These candid stories will give you peace and hope. They will give you the strength you need to get up off that couch and search for the joy you've always wanted.

As Ganel-Lyn says so profoundly, "If we approach adversities wisely, our hardest times can be times of greatest growth, which, in turn, can lead toward times of our greatest happiness." Thank you, Ganel-Lyn, for this compilation, a true testament of your work in helping all of us find joy in this life!

Life is not determined by
what happens to me,
but by how I respond to what happens.
It is not about what life brings to me
but what I bring to life.
—Anonymous

Introduction

REJOICING IS A LITERAL PROTECTION! It grows from gratitude no matter the circumstances. It is praising God when we are both happy and sad, peaceful and stressed, sure and doubtful. "Life is filled with detours and dead ends, trials and challenges of every kind. Each of us has likely had times when distress, anguish, and despair almost consumed us. Yet we are here to have joy? Yes! The answer is a resounding yes! But how is that possible? And what must we do to claim the joy that Heavenly Father has in store for us?"[4]

I remember listening to President Russell M. Nelson say these words in general conference close to the time it became clear that the With God book series was not complete. I had been pondering my next project and the word *joy*. I knew that what the world needed most was hope and joy. So many people around me had endured great challenges and loss. And the previous few years had been filled with some of the biggest tests and heartbreaks of my life. I could see the hand of God through the opposition—but I was missing something. I was missing the joy. So I decided *joy* would be my New Year's word for 2017.

With each new book project or speaking event, God allows me to be tutored on a principle before I can share anything about it. I realized that to compile a book about joy, I had better get focused on *choosing more joy* myself. I already kept a daily gratitude list, but I soon realized joy was a step above gratitude. So I focused on scriptures about joy, talks about joy, home décor with the word *joy* incorporated in it. I made a conscious choice to lean into the joy offered to me every day, even in the most trying circumstances.

I have come to know, as I have pondered and worked on this project, that joy is more than being happy. It has come to mean: a true sense of well-being, even when everything around you is in chaos. It is what the

4 Russell M. Nelson, "Joy and Spiritual Survival," *Ensign*, Nov. 2016.

scriptures say: "Adam fell that men might be; and men are, that they might have joy."[5] And men are that we *might* have joy. Might. If we choose to.

Some of the women in this book share vulnerable stories that may not seem fitting for a joy project. Yet as you read of their journeys, you will come to see the deep and powerful feelings of hope that have come from their choosing. These stories are beyond mere happiness. These warrior women have come to see God's hand leading them through difficult and disappointing conditions.

Along with these stories, I also wanted to include some over-the-top, miraculously joyful stories. You as readers will get updates from previous With God contributors. There have been some big changes in the lives of both Betsy Ferguson (*I Can Do Hard Things with God*) and Laryssa Waldron (*I Can Do Hard Things with God / The Decision That Changed My Life*). I guarantee you won't stop smiling when you read about their news.

And my own journey literally took me overseas. All of these experiences have born testimony, again, of God's great power and desire to bless His children.

What we focus on increases. As I have practiced choosing more joy, more has materialized. My son recently returned from serving a mission in Zimbabwe. Each week when he emailed stories of extreme poverty and corruption, I was overwhelmed by the joy of the people despite it all. The light in their eyes and the happiness in their smiles told me that having an easy life, the best house, the perfect job, or an efficient, honest government weren't requirements for choosing or experiencing joy. The Zimbabwe people are joyful because they choose to be.

Eliza R. Snow, second general president of the Relief Society, talked of the source of their joy after Missouri's infamous extermination order. It was the winter of 1838, and she and other Saints were forced to flee the state. There were eighty people crowded inside one small cabin, and many had to stand or sit all night because there was not room to lie down; they were only trying to keep warm. Some of the men spent the night gathered around a roaring fire while others sang hymns or roasted frozen potatoes. Eliza recorded: "Not a complaint was heard—all were cheerful, and judging from appearances, strangers would have taken us to be pleasure excursionists rather than a band of gubernatorial exiles." She declared, "That was a very merry night. None but saints can be happy under every circumstance."[6]

---

5 2 Nephi 2:25.

6 See Eliza R. Snow, in Edward W. Tullidge, *The Women of Mormondom* (1877), 145-46, quoted in Russell M. Nelson, "Joy and Spiritual Survival," *Ensign*, Nov. 2016.

The world needs joy. It is a protection from men's hearts failing them. Joy is possible, and if God commands that we *might have joy*, He will open the way to obey His commands. I hope and pray that these stories will infuse you with joy, inspire you to choose joy, and instigate your own joy journey. No matter what your circumstance may be, choose to pass through it *with God*.

Part I: Gifts

Chapter 1
God Moves Mountains: Mission to England
By Ganel-Lyn Condie

Monday, April 27, 2017, 2:13 p.m.

> *Brooklyn and I are on our way to England. Is this really happening? Am I really going to ENGLAND and taking my daughter with me? My God is a mighty God. He surely moves mountains. He moves them every day, but today, I must take notice. I am trying not to be too nervous. God has opened so many doors for me. He surely will sustain me and provide the words I am being sent to share with my brothers and sisters in England. I am thinking about Nephi, again . . .*

> And it came to pass that I, Ganel-Lyn, say unto the world: "I will go and do the things which the Lord hath commanded, for I know that the Lord giveth no commandments unto the children of men, save he shall prepare a way for them that they may accomplish the thing which he commandeth them."[7]

This English "mission" story began many months before, on an April day in the Salt Lake City Delta terminal. My Father in Heaven knows me perfectly. He knows He must warm me up to things. I need heart promptings and nudges to prepare me for the big commanding-revelation moments. So, it was in early 2016 that I first started to recognize those faint impressions about expanding the scope and reach of my mission. At the time, I was overcome with gratitude for the success of my first book, *I Can Do Hard Things with God.* How could it get any better?

Speaking events were steady and allowed me to connect with people and testify in a different way than writing. I was busy with a family, and though we

---

7 1 Nephi 3:7.

were still struggling financially, we were employed, and things were improving. Slowly. Our son, Cameron, was finishing his senior year, and talk of a mission and college was constant.

The calendar was always as full as I hoped it would be while still balancing my health and family. God was persistent in teaching me both personally and professionally. I was developing new spiritual muscles. I felt like I was working for God. I was busy at home and working outside the home.

So when the nudging began and I started to feel whispers (that is how I describe the Spirit's voice) in words and thoughts, I knew they were coming from the Source because they were beyond my usual ideas. The impression was that it was time to go farther from home. And the interesting thing about it was my patriarchal blessing stated that I would serve another kind of mission.

Occasionally, I was asked to travel out of state to share a message of faith and hope. But this time, God was telling me it was time to go to another country, across an ocean. But how? We barely had a budget for date nights, let alone a transatlantic trip. My husband had been nothing but supportive of this work—my long hours at the computer writing, speaking events that took me away from home. But what worried Rob the most was my health and keeping up with such a busy schedule. What would he say about these flashes of revelation?

I have tried to be what Elder Ronald A. Rasband calls "a first responder."[8] When I get a thought that leads me to do good, I try to act quickly. Personal revelation rarely comes in perfectly organized outlines or timelines. Instead, the Spirit trusts us with small lenses and steady streams of light that should lead to action on our part. But what could I do with these crazy thoughts of traveling to other countries to speak?

The promptings didn't consume me. They were just always floating in the back of my mind. I tried to be alert to opportunities that might lead to something else. And one day, I even thought about sponsorship. I had heard of benefactors. Maybe the Lord had a sponsor in my future. On another day, I considered what country He wanted me to visit. I thought of my sister living in Italy at the time. She had often said the women on her military base had read my books and would love to hear me speak. I told her I was always willing if she could find a way. Eventually, they were restationed back in the States. So I wouldn't be going to Italy!

---

8 "Let the Holy Spirit Guide," *Ensign*, May 2017.

Later, I remembered that I knew someone else living overseas. Kim Friend was an American whose family was working and living in Harrogate, England. Her family and I were in the same San Diego ward eighteen years earlier. Kim and her sisters looked like they could be my sisters, so everyone at church always assumed I was one of the Reinhart girls. I loved the Reinhart family and had fond memories of Sunday dinners and hummus. But Kim and I rarely communicated with each other. Thank goodness for Facebook, though, for shortening the miles. I found out she was currently serving as Relief Society president in her Harrogate ward.

One night, Kim and I were messaging about my books and my mission to share faith and hope, especially when it came to suicide. She mentioned wanting to get some of my books to give to women in her area. I told her I would work on it. In our book-shipping conversation, we talked of my speaking events, and I bravely shared the very personal, private promptings about speaking abroad. She said she would love to have me speak to her ward and I could stay with her.

I half jokingly said, "Okay, Kim, you start praying for a sponsor, and I won't stop praying for one."

"Deal!" Kim then shared that their time in England was coming to a close and they would be moving back to the States in May 2017. This was fall 2016, so if Kim was going to be my host, God needed to start working on a way.

Mountains Move Slowly

Because of my history with lupus, I do a lot of self-care and preventive health support. I can't afford to not put my health on my to-do list. I have a big tool-box of spiritual, emotional, and physical tools. I put everything and anything of value in the box. This includes personal coaching, massage, temple visits, sleep, exercise, priesthood blessings, and daily prayer and scripture study.

One day, I was at my friend Jenny Swim's home. I noticed this interesting tool sitting on the table that looked like a fancy, large electrical toothbrush. Instead of a toothbrush head, though, it had two adjustable arms. I instinctively picked it up and turned it on, running it over the top of my head and around my ears. It was an amazing circular, vibrating sensation. I was in the middle of a monthly migraine, and instantly, I not only felt relief from the headache pain but I also felt my nervous system calm, like when you are meditating or sleeping. I asked Jenny about it, and she said it was a Rezzimax Tuner and that they could be purchased online. For the rest of our visit, I used the Tuner.

Then I went home to investigate. I reached out to the owner/creator of the Tuner to see if I could do a profile about his tool and learn more about the creation process for my *Daily Herald* newspaper column. Sharik Peck enthusiastically sent me a Tuner for my own research, and we outlined a plan for interviews for the *Everyday Faith* piece. I used the Tuner on my kids to help them relax before bed. I used it on my tight jaw after nights of clenching my teeth. And, of course, it was amazing for headaches and anxiety. I did a phone interview with Sharik, looked over some of the technical materials, and wrote up the article.[9] I was so excited to share this new process with my loyal readers.

As the New Year circled around again, I looked at my upcoming calendar and pondered on my new goals. There were some exciting new opportunities as well as gaps in my plans—but I have learned to trust the gap times in my schedule. They end up being filled with unknown events, or they stay open for preparation and rest. As I looked, I noticed my spring was more open than usual. Specifically, April.

We celebrated the beginning of 2017 with the release of my new book and the article I had worked on about the Rezzimax Tuner. The Pecks were thrilled with the write-up and had also started buying copies of my books to give to neighbors and friends. They kept expressing appreciation for my writing style and how I had captured their story with heart.

In February, I was in the throes of book signings and speaking events. I had a large, multistake women's conference in Logan to speak at and a book signing afterward. The Pecks lived in Cache Valley, and since our communication had been via phone and email, they decided to come hear me speak and offered to take me to lunch as a thank-you for the newspaper column I had done.

I splurged on a cheap motel in Logan for the Friday night before the women's conference so I could be close to the church Saturday morning. At the motel, I took extra time in the scriptures and didn't rush my journaling time. Throughout it all, I had the reoccurring thought: *Does God really want me to go across the globe to share my message? And if so, how?*

I confess to being a bit more reflective around February. That is my birthday month, and I tend to take stock every February 1. On this occasion,

9 See http://www.heraldextra.com/momclick/home-and-garden/everyday-faith/
everyday-faith-tuning-your-body-to-joy/.

I went to Heavenly Father with some concerns. *Did He really want me to keep writing books and speaking? Was I doing all I could to care for my family? Was I making any difference in the world? And what should I start or stop doing?* I didn't ever want to lose focus on what this work was about and what was most important. I wanted to serve God, but I was old enough to know the greatest work was often done quietly in a baby's room and not in a boardroom or bookstore. If Heavenly Father wanted me to serve the way I had been, I needed to know that. I didn't want to get distracted with book sales or speaking events. I wanted this work to be about Him, not me.

As I finished my prayer that night and crawled into the stiff motel sheets, I had the thought, *Maybe God doesn't really want me to go across the world to speak. Maybe He was just seeing if I would be willing, you know, like an Abrahamic sacrifice.*

February was ending. There were no sponsors on the horizon. The Friend family would be back in America soon. Maybe it wasn't meant to be.

God must have known I was willing to risk for Him. I had tried to show it each time I spoke to a group or paid the bills or started another book. I always tried to keep at least one toe out of my comfort zone as a token of my dedication to living a faith-based life. But I confess to feeling a bit released from the original prompting or need to travel that night. I had some anxiety about being away from home too much. And financially, I wasn't sure how I could ask more of our budget. It felt good to finally let go of some of that pressure there in the motel room. I went to sleep with snow falling outside, resting in the thought that I had tried to find a way to follow God's command for me—but it must have just been a *test* to see if I was willing. Test passed.

A MOUNTAINOUS SHIFT

I woke up a bit early so I'd have the morning to prepare for my long day of speaking, my lunch appointment with the Pecks, the book signing, and the drive back to Lehi. After getting ready and before leaving for the conference, I checked Facebook. I had a message request, which meant it had come from someone who wasn't one of my Facebook friends. I opened it to read the following message:

Saturday, February 11, 2017, 8:04 a.m.

Hi! I really hope you don't mind me messaging you? I am in the same ward as Kim Friend, and after I'd gone through some pretty horrible experiences, she gave me your book *I Can Do Hard Things with God*. That was about three weeks ago. My family had been inactive in the Church for about a year after feeling like Heavenly Father had just abandoned us. I wanted to thank you. Your book has helped me so, so much. My husband is currently reading it, and we are back at church. And it just feels like we aren't alone in suffering and we definitely haven't been abandoned. So, thank you again. *I hope we can meet someday.*

xoxo, Rebecca Waring (Harrogate, England)

As I read Rebecca's heartfelt message, the Spirit washed over me, and my eyes filled with tears.

And then very clearly, I heard the words, "You are still going to England. It wasn't just to see if you would be willing."

I looked around because, while the words were in my heart, they were so powerful that I thought they might have been spoken. It was an undeniable message. Once again, I thought of Nephi: "For I know that the Lord giveth no commandments unto the children of men, save he shall prepare a way for them that they may accomplish the thing which he commandeth them."[10]

That cheap little motel room felt as bright as a room in the temple. The Spirit was thick, and my tears flowed. Not only had I heard heaven speak, but I also felt like my pleading and wondering about doing any good in the world was once again quieted. Rebecca's message was an addition to my collection of "For the One" letters. I call them "For the One" because they are letters/messages I have received from people who have been supported or touched in some way by a talk I have given or by one of the books I have written. I call them "For the One" because I say, "I would do it all again for that *one*!" Rebecca Waring from Harrogate, England, was on the top of my For-the-One stack.

The multistake women's conference went well. God loves His daughters. I feel it every time I speak to a group of women or young women. That February morning was no different. The stake center was filled all the way to the back of the cultural hall. I wondered if I would be able to spot Sharik and his wife, Cheryl, to meet up for our lunch appointment. But during the break, I found them in the foyer waiting for me to finish greeting and hugging women from the conference. We decided to eat at the world-famous Blue Bird Café.

---

10 1 Nephi 3:7.

Lunch was nice. It was one of those first-time meetings that felt more like a reunion. We ordered our food and chatted about the basics of life. They were complimentary about the message I had shared at the conference. I gave the glory to God. I told them I couldn't have done the hundreds of speaking events I'd done if it weren't about Him and for Him.

The Pecks totally got it. They live their lives the same way. They shared some amazing miracle stories about the Tuner and those it had helped. They stopped and then said, "We would do it all again, all the sacrifice, all the struggle, for that one person." *For the one!* Then they said, "I bet you feel the same way about your books and speaking."

I paused. Then I told them of the newest message I had received from Rebecca.

As I related the story, including the books and the Facebook communication I'd had with Kim, I heard that familiar Spirit-voice speak once again, clearly, to my mind and heart. "These people are going to offer to sponsor you." It was so clear that I panicked.

I immediately thought of my daughter.

There was no way they would offer to sponsor us both, and with her brother (and best friend) gone in Zimbabwe, I couldn't leave her home right now. But the impressions were so clear and my panicked mother mind so busy that I thought I would talk the Pecks out of the sponsorship *before* they even offered it. Immediately after sharing Rebecca's message, I brought up how I try to not be gone from home too much, especially with Brooklyn home alone now.

We finished our lunch. I headed to the book signing, and so did they. True to their word, they bought another pile of books for friends and neighbors who were in need of some support. I loved meeting the Pecks. After knowing their story and journey in creating the Rezzimax Tuner and learning more about their desire to just help people, I felt an instant familial bond with the Pecks. These were good people trying to live out of their comfort zone, serve God, and help their fellow man. Their mission was similar to mine.

On the drive home, I pondered the new information—I would say revelation—I had received in just the past two days. Once again, my doubt had been overcome by grace. No matter what my future travel plans were or book sales or experiences, I had felt God's hand directing my life. He cared about what I cared about, and He would always be there, no matter what.

✦ ✦ ✦

Tuesday February 14, 2017, 9:25 a.m.

Ganel-Lyn, Cheryl and I feel like we need to help you and your daughter get to England to help the good people there. They need the message of hope and healing through our Savior that you can provide. Please let us know what you need to make this happen.

—Sharik Peck

What did I just read in my Facebook message?
What did that say?
Help you and your daughter get to England!
Tears immediately dripped onto my computer keyboard.

Once again, I'd been taught. My God is a mighty God. He can move mighty mountains.

All types of feelings and emotions flooded my heart. Could this really be true? How had my Father in Heaven made this miracle happen? Was I worthy? Would I be able to deliver the right message?

Pure joy overtook the questions. Over a year ago, the feelings and thoughts the Spirit had planted in my heart had seemed impossible. Now those impressions had matured to become consistent messages and actions coming to pass. I had been compelled to keep the idea of traveling far from home clear in my mind and to act when prompted to. I had searched and pondered and prayed to know how and where. And just when I thought the chance had passed, this happened!

Soon my joy was overcome with a gripping fear.

What did the Pecks expect from me? Did they want me to promise lifelong servitude? Did they really mean to help get both Brooklyn and me to England? I knew what the cost was. I had been searching for flight deals overseas for close to twelve months. It would not be a small price tag. They barely knew me, and I knew only a small part of their life. This could be a recipe for disaster. Unmet expectations and resentment had ruined potentially great partnerships in the past. I didn't want that.

I immediately sent a message back to Sharik. I thanked him and expressed how truly overwhelmed I was by his offer. Clarifying conversations continued between us for a few days. In the end, the Pecks reassured me that they were only following a direct-command prompting from God to offer this sponsor-ship and they expected nothing in return. Truly, angels walk the earth today.

I reached out to Kim Friend immediately to tell her our prayers had been answered. God had provided an Amulek for this Alma. We had a sponsor. She was thrilled. We then started the complicated process of scheduling firesides, looking at Brooklyn's school schedule, and checking airfare. With English schools' spring break running two full weeks in April and the Friend family's scheduled move back to the U.S. in May, our window was narrowing. Kim joyfully reassured me that she would walk me through all the travel details and help take care of us once we arrived. For a girl who has mild travel anxiety, I was comforted.

A few weeks following their initial offer, Cheryl and Sharik came to our Lehi home to finalize the tickets. As we invited the Pecks into our living room, I asked if we could have a quick prayer. Even after all their reassuring, I was nervous about expectations and feelings of regret creeping in. After the prayer, I turned to Sharik and Cheryl and said how grateful I was that they had followed such a profound prompting. I asked them if they were sure they wanted to or even could do this.

Cheryl said, "Are you asking if we have the money to do this—well, the answer is no. But we are doing this. We have committed to doing as God commands, and He wants this trip to happen. He wants you to speak to the Saints in England." She then went on to testify that Heavenly Father has always provided for them and has never let them go without. Sharik then shared similar thoughts. He expounded on how the money was always there and even went on to say that a client he had been trying to get under contract for over a year for physical therapy consulting contacted them the day after they had sent me the offer, saying they were ready to sign. Sharik said that alone would cover the costs and was a sign that God would provide. They were determined to do this.

Rob shared how overwhelmed he was and said he felt inspired to act in a similar way in the future.

The Pecks were remarkable. They were truly dedicated to living a God-directed life, with the understanding that when God commanded, He opened the way. They felt, as I did, that this trip was a command. They were not going to ignore a message from Father in Heaven, so neither was I.

We bought the tickets and just as the Pecks were about to leave, Cheryl made a comment about a genealogy issue she had. She turned to Sharik and said, "Maybe Ganel-Lyn can help us find Ann's parents when she is in

England." Cheryl had gotten stuck on one of her ancestors who had lived in England. She couldn't find record of the woman's parents. No birth certificates or marriage records. I felt a warm swelling fill my chest as I said, "Send me the information, Cheryl. If God has gotten us this far *and* all the way to England, He surely can help with a genealogy issue."

In the coming days, we rushed to amend Brooklyn's expired passport and started making plans. Quickly, a fireside in the York Stake took form. I would speak on Sunday to the Saints in this beautiful part of the country. Word got out that I was coming, and soon, a second fireside was scheduled in the Sunderland Stake. We were planning to be in England for only a week. Actually, six days. I was nervous about being jet lagged, about how my health and body would hold up, and about how Brooklyn would do. Each time I started to get overwhelmed with travel details or feelings of inadequacy, I would remember the scripture in 1 Nephi, and feelings of joy would overtake me. This was really happening. God had worked a mighty miracle to get to this point. He would not let me fail now.

Kim was a great help. With the time difference and her late-night instant-messaging availability, I asked every European travel question I could think of—from hair dryers to train rides into London. Kim walked me through it all. And when my head wasn't swimming with travel concerns, I would ponder on the messages I was to share. One day, a friend offhandedly commented that having a sponsor was a lot of pressure and I better be worth it. Like I didn't know that already.

One of the great blessings of this mission trip was watching Brooklyn. She had gone through the same two job losses I had. My children had never complained about missed vacations and minimal spending. My son had saved his own money to pay for his mission, and my daughter never asked for anything she didn't think she could buy with her own babysitting money. I agreed with the Pecks—this trip was just as much about Brooklyn's life mission and development as it was my mission. Maybe even more so. I felt more joy just watching her excitement and anticipation than I did experiencing my own. In between firesides and visiting the locally owned LDS bookstore to sign a few books, Brooklyn and I were going to take a train into London to Kings Cross! Platform 9 ¾ was a must-see.

I kept pinching myself. For real. Was I really going to travel over the ocean with my thirteen-year-old daughter, give two firesides, and take a train ride to London? God really did trust me more than I trusted myself. My missionary son was a huge help during this time. Every time I started to feel overwhelmed and like I was cracking emotionally, I thought of my boy. Elder Cameron Condie was a nineteen-year-old from Lehi, Utah, living in Zimbabwe! He lived in extreme poverty. He washed his own clothes in a bucket. He sometimes went without electricity, and he walked miles in the heat every day. If Cameron could leave everything familiar and comfortable to live in Africa for two years and serve the Lord, I could do a week in England with a host family who wouldn't let me starve or be stranded.

This entire experience was sacred to me. The initial promptings. The interview for the Rezzimax Tuner. The message from Rebecca. The sponsorship. All of it felt so precious to me that for a few weeks, only a very few people even knew I was going to England. Then on March 22, a terrorist attack happened in London, near the British Parliament. A Utah man, Kurt Cochran, was hit by the car the terrorist was driving and died. It was time to announce my trip. Wicked must not win. I wanted to tell the world I wasn't afraid to go to London. Now, more than ever, I wanted to share love and hope with my brothers and sisters in England. Not fear.

Mountains Moved

> Monday, April 27, 2017, 2:13 p.m.
>
> With our Rezzimax sweatshirts on, we board the Delta plane and take our seats. I start to cry. I can't stop the tears. They keep coming because now I see that there are fourteen new missionaries heading into the field on our flight. I feel and share their anxiety. I see the excitement in their eyes. I am right there with them. We buckle our seat belts, and I reach over to squeeze my wide-eyed daughter's hand. I whisper, "Brooklyn, we are going to England! Can you believe it?

There were too many amazing encounters to count. But they all started with sharing a copy of one of my books with a Muslim woman living in Leeds. We saw beautiful countryside. Sheep and green pastures. Old stone walls and small towns draped with flags and spring flowers. We met shopkeepers and toured an old abbey. But most of all, we met and loved the people. The Friend family became our family for the week. They were generous hosts and worked hard to help us fight jet lag and have what we needed. Kim was my chauffeur and impressed us with her Mario Andrade driving skills. I never quite got used to the other side of the car and the other side of the road.

As I walked into the Sunderland stake center, I at once felt the room was filled with angels seen and unseen. The front two pews were filled with full-time missionaries serving in the area. Love overwhelmed any feelings of nerves. These boys were like my boy. They were away from home and family. They were learning to live with strangers and love investigators. I prayed quickly that something I shared would bless them.

As I walked to the podium, I surrendered. This was God's work. This moment wasn't about me. He sent me here to share a message. My job was to get out of the way and hear what words needed to be said. As I spoke, I prayed that the Atonement of Christ would cover any mistakes I made. After I sat down, I breathed in the air and the feelings in the room. I never wanted to forget this night. I could see elders along the front row overcome with emotion. Something I'd said had touched their hearts. The stake center was filled with Saints I had never met until that night, but they felt like my brothers and sisters now. Looking out on the them, I could sense their hearts were open. They had come with questions. And prayers had been answered.

After the closing prayer, members came to meet and greet. We hugged, and we cried. Missionaries expressed how the message had helped them with personal feelings of doubt and struggle with the mission. They thanked me for helping them stay and work. Then I noticed a young father standing off to the side of the chapel with his pregnant wife and toddler-aged son. He was patiently waiting for the other members to finish their hugs and thanksgiving. He quietly approached and hugged me, with tears streaming down his face. He shared with me that he had just survived a suicide attempt and that he knew God had sent me there just for him. He thanked me, and I kept telling him it was his Father in Heaven. God had a work for him to do, and he must fight to stay in his body until his mission on earth was complete. I was overcome with love for this humble man. He was in a real struggle, one I had seen hundreds of times at many firesides.

As Kim and I said our goodbyes and made our way home to Harrogate, I tried to process with her the complex feelings I was having. It was almost more than I could take in. If I had come for the one—that one missionary, that one father, that one sister confined to her wheelchair—this was all worth it. As I prayed to my Father, I thanked Him for all the mountains that had been moved so this night could be. I pleaded for those missionaries and that father who now had a second chance to live. I prayed for my own missionary, asking that someone would come into his life to lift his weary arms.

Brooklyn and I made our way to London. We saw as much as we could squeeze into a day. Then we headed back to Harrogate. Saturday was amazing as we attended the Preston Temple and visited the LDS bookstore. The shopkeepers were so surprised to see an American author walk into the store that day.

* * *

Kim and I had talked briefly about the Peck's genealogy issue, Ann's missing parents. She said there happened to be an amazing genealogist in her ward and we would try to talk with him on Sunday. Of course there was! Sunday arrived, and I happened to sit in front of this genealogy wiz in Sunday School. Kim introduced us and explained the dilemma. He promised to meet with her the following Tuesday evening at the church library to see if he could help the Pecks. This week had gone so fast. To think of all the promptings, prayers, and planning that had made this week happen! I didn't want it to end. I went for a walk around the city park. I drank in all the aging architecture, the trees, and the smells. I didn't want any cell in my body to forget how God had moved a mountain in my life.

As I we prepared to leave for the York stake center, I struggled, realizing we would be going home early the next morning. I loved being home, but now I felt a part of me would always be in England. We entered the York chapel and watched as the pews filled one by one. Some Saints had driven over three hours to attend this fireside, and others had taken a train and would stay overnight just to be a part of this event. I pleaded with God on behalf of these dear people once more. "Please, Father, help me say what you would have me say. Nothing more!"

As I made my way back to my seat on the stand after having delivered the message, I felt angels surrounding me. God had kept His promises. He had commanded me to go. He had directed me to speak. He had reassured me that I would be sustained. What He had asked, He had delivered. I had just needed to be willing.

As the stake president closed the meeting and the prayer was said, I took a deep breath in and out. It was complete. I hugged hundreds of my sisters and brothers that night. I met women from Zimbabwe. I met nonmembers who were meeting with the missionaries. I met women who were divorced and tired. I met leaders. I met families. We cried and hugged and took a lot of pictures.

As Brooklyn and I climbed into bed that night, she said, "Mom, I have never heard you speak like that. It was awesome."

I said, "Brooklyn, God is the awesome one. He did this."

* * *

Monday, April 24, 2017, 12:45 p.m.

We made it home. Rob was thrilled to have us back, espe-
cially since it was his 49th birthday. We unpacked, had some
takeout, sang a little happy birthday, and were asleep by 4:30
p.m. Utah time. Tuesday morning was a regular school day
for Brooklyn. She couldn't afford to miss any more school. Rob
was back at work, and I was trying to record my final journal
entry from the trip. I didn't want to forget any details or faces.

Later that afternoon as I sat at the computer getting some work done, Kim popped up on Google Hangouts. She was at the Church working on the genealogy mystery.

This was our instant message conversation:

Kim: We found Ann Roe Pell's parents!

Ganel-Lyn: WHAT-WHAT-WHAT-WHAT!?! I am crying—a lot!

Kim: We've even found a marriage certificate and are working on birth certificates now.

Ganel-Lyn: Kim—can you believe the miracles from this trip?? If you wonder if there is a God or if He cares about the one, just remember this day! Please hug that sweet man for me!

Kim: By the way, their names are Thomas Roe and Ann Bottamley.

As soon as Kim and I finished our conversation, I called the Pecks. I couldn't contain my joy. I cried, and they waited patiently for me to speak.

"Cheryl, you won't believe what just happened! They found Ann's parents. Kim found them!" Silence on the other end told me I was no longer crying alone. As soon as I could talk, I said, "Why should it surprise us? God cares just as much about the families on that side of the veil as He does the families on this side of the veil. It is no big deal for Him to get a mom from Utah over to England if it means sealing a family for eternity. Even if He has to start working on it many years before."

Within a week of Brooklyn and me coming home, the temple work for Ann's family had been started and completed. Cheryl and Sharik texted me a picture in front of the Logan Temple, holding the family file cards. As I considered the immense joy I was feeling, the thought came to me that my capacity had grown. I had experienced some extreme opposition and adversity over the past few years. But the law of opposition is that as our capacity to feel sorrow increases, so does our capacity to feel joy. I felt like my heart might burst open.

No matter what messages I shared at those English firesides, no matter what impact I have on readers of my books, I helped in a small way to bring Ann's family together forever. The joy I felt from that miracle was almost more than words could describe.

The miracles didn't stop after the bags and souvenirs were unpacked. Two notable miracles involve the Pecks and Rebecca. One day, a month after coming home, I got a call from Cheryl and Sharik. They had some news to share. Sharik had been approached about going to Ecuador to do a humanitarian mission and to train nurses on the Tuner. The organizer of the trip said he thought they could secure a sponsorship to allow Sharik and even his daughter to go. In the end, someone provided money for both of them to go to Ecuador to teach teams of medical professionals about the Tuner. And the cost of the two tickets for both Sharik and his daughter equaled almost to the dollar what the Pecks had used to sponsor Brooklyn and me to go to England. Another mountain moved.

> Sunday, July 9, 2017, 10:24 a.m.
>
> I wanted to share with you that I got my temple recommend renewed today! Your book helped me see that I needed to return to church, and now I'm returning to the temple with Will! I'll be eternally grateful.
>
> —Rebecca Waring (Harrogate, England)

I have heard it said that it really is always about families and the temple. No matter what comes, when those moments of doubt overwhelm me, I will remember England. When I am paralyzed with uncertainty about how I will be able to do what has been asked or commanded, I will remember when God moved many mighty mountains and sent me to England with my daughter.

* * *

I share this sacred story not to share a fanciful experience but in hopes that you will begin to recognize what God has planted in your heart, for you to believe for a moment that He isn't just capable of moving mountains; He is motivated to.

What messages does He keep whispering to your mind?

I pray that as you finish reading about this mini-mission, my journey across the pond, you will never doubt what God can do, especially when He has asked it of you. He has already planned for your success. Your Father in Heaven will move both the big and small mountains. I promise you that— because He did it and continues to do it for me every day.

Chapter 2
Unexpected Gifts: An Adoption Story
By Kathryn Jenkins

THE DAY WE HAD EAGERLY awaited was finally here: our birth mother was in labor at the hospital, and we were at home, pacing nervously like the expectant parents we were. This baby, just beginning the physical struggle that would bring her into mortality, was a girl—exactly what we had hoped for and a perfect complement to our daughter and two sons. She was also half African-American, exactly like our other three adopted children.

Things couldn't have been more perfect.

Until they weren't.

Partway through the long process of giving birth to her first baby, the young woman with whom we had been working for months started having second thoughts. The phone call came from our contact, warning us. Trying to prepare us. *She's really feeling unsure of her decision; this might not go as expected.*

My stomach churned.

Why now? For months, she had been so sure. Had felt so good about it. Had felt so good about *us*. We had felt so good about *her*. We had cautiously but confidently prepared to welcome her baby into our home. Our family. We had poured out our gratitude to our Heavenly Father.

And now this.

I catapulted back and forth between feelings of mind-numbing dread and a refusal to consider that we might lose this baby. *This can't be happening.* I clung to shreds of hope. I wandered again and again into the nursery we had prepared, clutching a soft flannel receiving blanket, white knuckled.

Mostly, I prayed. I dropped to my knees what seemed like every few minutes. I asked that angels surround that little mother who was laboring with all her might to accomplish birth. But more than that, I pleaded that all would go as planned and that within a few days, *I* would hold that new little girl in *my* arms, pressed against *my* heart.

It was what I wanted. What I dreamed about. What I hoped for. What I had planned for.

The hours of her labor dragged by. She just couldn't change her mind. Not now. I was never far from the phone. Our other three children—the oldest almost six, the youngest almost two—played with carefree abandon, never realizing the gut-wrenching battle that raged in my heart and mind and spirit.

At last, we received the call. She had arrived—a perfect, healthy little girl, seven pounds, a head full of silky black curls. "You need to know . . . her mother has been holding her. Wants to breastfeed her. Has named her. She still has a few days to decide, but I'm not sure she's going to surrender this baby."

There were no words. No words for the despair that slammed into me.

Now my prayers were almost constant—pleading, entreating, petitioning. *Please, Father. Oh, please, Father.* I begged. I implored. I stopped just shy of demanding because even in my desperation, I knew I could not demand *anything* of a Father who was aware of even the smallest sparrow. Surely, He knew my heart. Clearly, He would not deny me this.

I couldn't eat. Couldn't sleep. Nothing—not even the attempts of my husband to settle my anguish—brought me comfort.

Me, me, me. In the scarce moments of clarity that pushed their way through my frantic mind, I realized there was another woman—one who was young and alone and uncertain—whose prayers were also undoubtedly winging their way heavenward. What was *she* feeling? What words formed *her* supplications?

The hours seemed to crawl. One day, then two. No word.

I was a wreck.

Very early on the third morning, sometime before the sun began to tickle the sky, something happened to my beleaguered heart. *This isn't about me. It's about a mother and her baby and the plan of a loving Father.* For the first time since my frenetic imploring had started three days earlier, I slid out of bed and offered a prayer unlike any I had uttered through those desperate hours.

He knew how desperately I wanted this baby. He knew every crevice and corner of my heart, even better than *I* knew them. But I finally managed the courage to voice what I should have been saying all along: *Thy will, not mine, be done.*

I slid back into bed, gathered my grandmother's hand-stitched quilt around my shoulders, and fell into a deep and quenching sleep.

It was still early when the phone rang. I clawed my way out of the depths of a scattered dream and snatched the phone from its cradle. "I'm so sorry. She just left the hospital, and she took the baby home with her. She just couldn't do it. She asked me to tell you how sorry she is."

Sorry. It seemed so feeble. All the hopes, all the dreams, all of it crashed around me with sickening finality. This was more than *sorry.*

But there it was: *Thy will, not mine, be done.* I didn't understand. But *He* did. He knew everything, the beginning from the end. My job now was clear—to accept His will. To move on. To pack up the receiving blankets and frilly dresses and pink sleepers and hand-crocheted booties. To quiet the name *I* had given her without even seeing her.

To be okay.

And to my astonishment, I was. Much sooner than I thought I would be.

And then came the twist I never would have imagined. This time, I didn't get a call. I saw it in the newspaper. Two weeks from the day she was born, that tiny little girl cut the tethers binding her to mortality and soared back to the Father who had given her life.

"Sudden Infant Death Syndrome," the obituary said.

Just like that, she was gone.

I dropped to my knees again, this time in humility and with gratitude and amazement. My loving Father—yes, the same One who knows the beginning from the end, who knows even the smallest sparrow—knew all along that little soul would be here only a short time. He knew she would come just long enough to receive a body and that He would welcome her back into His arms in just the whisper of a moment.

And He knew, above all, that I would have been devastated to find her cold and still.

From the time I first became a mother, the menace of SIDS had terrified me. Our first baby—born two months early and weighing a mere three pounds—was incredibly fragile when we finally brought her home nearly a month after her birth. Still not quite five pounds, she couldn't maintain her own body temperature. She had to sleep under a heat lamp, and we had to take her temperature every few hours and make any necessary adjustments. She also didn't have a normal hunger drive; we had to set an alarm to make sure she didn't go longer than five hours without eating. Even then, she suckled only a few tablespoons of formula with each feeding. I remembered with dread the cold November night when that alarm went off—the first time she had actually slept past her feeding time. I sat up and screamed in terror, "The baby's dead! The baby's dead!"

She wasn't.

I crept into her room for months to listen for her soft breathing, putting my ear almost flush against her mouth when I couldn't hear it right away. Even prodding her awake a time or two when I wasn't sure.

Our two sons, who came later, were both older when we adopted them— one eighteen months, the other twenty-two months—and were well past the general risk for SIDS. They were solidly *here*, with little chance of leaving.

Now, in the most unexpected way, I was face-to-face with my greatest fear: a syndrome that silently crept into a crib and stole away an innocent babe. I was sorry beyond belief that the other mother had to experience such horror. At the same time, I was grateful beyond belief that *I* hadn't been asked to walk that path.

I was grateful to have been spared.

And I realized anew that everything works out when it is in the hands of Him who knows what is best for each of us.

Another Chance: Could I Do It?

Only a few months later, it happened again: word of another birth mother, another opportunity to welcome a baby into our family.

Did I have the courage to try?

Yes—a million times yes! I threw myself into this new possibility. As much as I rationally knew I should exercise caution, I allowed my heart to race ahead. In my mind's eye, I could see it all. And it was glorious.

Months went by. The time drew near. Again, I hoped. Dreamed. Grew restless with excited anticipation.

This time, we worked directly with the birth mother. No go-between. It was going to be an open adoption in which the birth mother (and other members of her family) would maintain contact with the child as he grew. The amount of contact varied from one situation to another, but we weren't concerned. We had open adoptions with our two boys, and those arrangements were working well. We had no reason to think it would be a problem in this case.

It wasn't. At least not for us. And not for her.

But it was a *big* problem for the mother's father.

This child, like our others, was half African-American. A joy for us, but not for this man who struggled with racism. Just four weeks before his daughter's due date, he issued an ultimatum: if she didn't go through an agency and have a traditional sealed adoption, he would disown her.

Disown her. I didn't even know that really happened in this day and age.

But he was serious. He didn't want the chance of a mixed-race child showing up on his porch and calling him *grandpa.*

The birth mother was mortified when she called us on that sweltering July afternoon. She couldn't financially *or* emotionally afford to be cut off from her parents. We certainly understood. She had decided to place her baby through LDS Social Services.

We were frantic. For months, we had worked with her. Planned. Prayed. We were *sure* she had *our* baby. And now *this.* Not crib death, certainly; no one had stopped breathing, but we felt the gripping cessation of life anyway.

That night, we sat in our bishop's office hoping for counsel that would ease our minds and hearts. His suggestion seemed ludicrous at first. "If you feel certain this is your baby, you need to go to LDS Social Services and explain the situation," he said. "I will call first thing in the morning as your bishop, and you should go in tomorrow." Then came the promise: "If you will do everything in your power to get this baby, I promise you will either get the baby, or you will have peace of mind."

The race was on.

The baby was due in four weeks.

We had heard horror stories about the kind of paperwork and bureaucracy that were part and parcel of adoption agencies. We were in a race, not just against time but against so many things that could go wrong.

That wasn't all. At the time, LDS Social Services had a carved-in-granite policy: they placed no more than two babies with any couple. And they never placed a baby with a couple that already had more than one child.

We had three.

It wasn't looking good for us.

Still, sailing on the promise of our bishop, we showed up.

LDS Social Services could not have been kinder or more accommodating. There was a lot of paperwork and bureaucracy, all right. The application process alone was daunting. And then there were the home studies—three of them, to be exact. They were supposed to be done over a period of months, but considering our time crunch (to put it mildly), they completed our three home studies in three weeks.

Everything was in place. They didn't say anything about the number of children we had, and there was no guarantee that anything would come of this. We were in the running for this baby just like everyone else now. They were clear there were no guarantees.

And so we waited, knowing their restrictions.

And we prayed.

My prayers this time were just as imploring, but I had learned a critical lesson from that last shattering experience. With every heart-wrenching appeal, I added the sincere caveat, *Thy will, not mine, be done.*

I trusted. I have to honestly say it did not come easily to me, but I trusted.

At the end of August, nearly a week after the baby was due, we got the call. "The baby was born," our social worker said, "and he's a little boy. We placed him with another family. But we think you're a great family, and we are going to keep your information on file."

Oh, sure, I thought. *We already have three children; we're not the family for you.*

But despite the disappointment, despite feeling almost resigned, I found, to my astonishment, that the bishop was right. Almost immediately, I felt complete peace of mind.

It was okay.

Everything was okay.

With the promised peace, I was able to put the experience out of my mind. *Far* out of my mind.

Little did I know that He who orders the universe was even then working behind the scenes to arrange a miracle that surpassed anything I could have imagined.

"You Have a Baby Boy"

Almost four months later, on a late Friday afternoon, I was racing around the house, trying to get my children ready for a family Christmas party—a dicey proposition with a six-year-old and two very active preschoolers. My husband was at work, driving for our local transit authority, when the phone rang.

I almost didn't answer but thought it might be my mother-in-law with a last-minute request.

It wasn't.

And who it was absolutely stunned me.

The social worker from LDS Social Services who had so kindly helped us four months earlier identified herself. That whole experience was so far out of my mind that at first I didn't register who she was.

She asked for my husband, and I explained that he was driving a city bus.

"Oh," she said, "then you get to tell him the happy news. You have a baby boy!"

Time absolutely stood still, just like it does in the movies.

My jaw dropped. My heart seemed to stop.

As I stood there in some sort of suspended animation, the details came flooding in. The birth mother was French/Italian. The birth father was African-American. The baby had been born in Houston on November 17. He had been placed in an LDS foster home and was awaiting all the necessary paperwork and clearance to be taken out of the state of Texas. They had named him Joey, and he loved kisses. It looked like he would arrive in Utah within the next week.

"Do you have any questions?"

Questions? I was still in shock.

"Congratulations! We'll be in touch."

By the time my wonderful neighbor had driven wildly along my husband's bus route while I waited anxiously by the phone to tell him the news once he found a phone and called me so I could relay the astonishing news to him, the local LDS Social Services office had closed for the weekend. We had questions, all right, but had to wait until Monday to get any answers.

What we learned on Monday was amazing. Rose, a twenty-one-year-old Catholic active in her faith, had been sent to Houston to live with her aunt during much of her pregnancy to avoid embarrassment to her family. While there, she went to Catholic Charities to start the process of arranging for placement of her baby.

But she didn't feel good about what they offered.

Rose's fervent hope was that her baby be raised with a testimony of the Savior. She didn't feel Catholic Charities could guarantee that.

She started the gritty process of going from one adoption agency to another, relying on prayer and gut instinct and steadily fraying hope to find the one where she felt comfortable placing her baby.

That was when she found it: LDS Social Services. Even knowing that her baby would be raised a member of The Church of Jesus Christ of Latter-day Saints, and not Catholic, she couldn't abandon her determination that he be given every chance to know Jesus Christ.

So there she was, at LDS Social Services. And there we were, at LDS Social Services. Something that, for all intents and purposes, never should have happened—and *wouldn't* have happened had it not been for that experience in August.

You know the one—the one we thought at the time was nothing more than an exercise in futility.

Only it wasn't. Not even close. It was the Lord's way of getting us into LDS Social Services—which we never would have considered—so all our paperwork would be in place and we would be there with open arms when Rose placed her precious baby there. Our social worker later told us that if we knew all the circumstances that had come together for the placement, there would be no doubt in our hearts that he was *our* son.

The next week was a whirlwind of activity as we got ready for our new little boy. The divine coincidences continued. The day our little boy was cleared to leave the state of Texas happened to be the same day Rose's social worker had airline tickets to fly his own family from Houston to Seattle for Christmas. Those tickets, purchased nine months earlier, included a two-hour layover in Salt Lake City.

And so it was that Paul Ricks bundled our baby up and hand-delivered him to the Salt Lake International Airport on December 21, 1986. Back in the day when you could wait for arriving passengers at the gate, we stood with *our* social worker, Beverly Edwards, watching eagerly as incoming passengers streamed off the plane. She had told Paul we'd be there to meet him: "I'll be the one in the red parka. I'll be with the nervous couple."

We waited. And watched. And waited. And watched.

Finally, when it seemed the plane must have completely emptied, he came through the door, our little boy pressed against his chest and covered with a flannel receiving blanket. He strode right up to us, lowered the baby, and asked, "And who should I give *this* little bundle to?"

Looking at the photos from that night still transports me. Jessica, who was six, couldn't stop kissing her little brother; we can't see his face in any of the pictures because she's in the way in every single one. We were surrounded—not only by all our family, including grandparents and great-grandparents, but by throngs of strangers who pressed in to share in the miracle, tears streaming down their cheeks. He was the best Christmas present ever. And to honor the Saint of that season, we named him Nicholas Jon—his middle name, Jon, in honor of Jon Stephens, the inspired bishop who sent us to LDS Social Services that day.

MORE THAN I EVER DREAMED

In so many ways, that little boy grew to become a man who is more than I ever could have dreamed. As a child, his imagination was incredible; he wrote and illustrated stories and used to stand in front of the stereo, holding a chopstick, pretending to conduct the orchestra. I often remarked that you could confine Nicholas in a four-by-four cement cell and he could still entertain himself for hours.

He saw and appreciated things the rest of us never noticed. He loved with reckless abandon, and so many loved him. He laughed with giggles that seemed to originate in his toes and brought more joy to our home than any of us ever knew existed.

He learned to play the violin and the cello and filled our home with unrivaled beauty. He starred in plays and musicals and even sang his heart out in a leading role in *Les Miserables*. He overcame tremendous obstacles with his health and some family tragedies to serve an honorable mission in Raleigh, North Carolina, where he tracted out and baptized a Methodist minister just a few months into his mission. And he set his course with resolve I've rarely seen to earn two bachelor's degrees from the University of Utah.

And Rose's desire that he grow to have a testimony of the Savior?

Oh, that desire was filled to capacity and so much more. Filled to overflowing.

I will never forget the day he and I were on our way to an appointment. I was darting through heavy traffic, and he was in a car seat in the back. Suddenly, tears started splashing down his cheeks, and he told me how much he missed Heavenly Father.

"Oh, I miss Him too," I said. "But you know that you can always talk to Him when you say your prayers, don't you?"

"Oh, I know, Mama. I *do* talk to Him, and He talks back."

A bit surprised, I asked a question I scarcely dared voice: "What does He say?"

From the heart of a three-year-old came words far above his level: "He says, 'Fear not, my child, for though you shall die, yet you shall live in me through my Son.' Isn't that good, Mama?"

So good, child. *So good.*

When Nicholas was thirteen, I took him to the temple with me to do baptisms for the dead. He went first, and as he emerged from the font, the temple workers wrapped him in a white towel and steered him toward the locker room. He asked if he could stay there and watch me. They seemed puzzled and a bit reluctant but agreed. He stood there, the water pooling around his bare feet, while I went next.

I entered the font and served as proxy for my grandmother—who had died when my father was nine—and my two aunts, women I scarcely knew. As I climbed the steps out of the font, Nicholas wrapped his arms around me and cried, "Oh, Mama, there were angels! There were angels!"

He knew his Father, and he knew his Savior. And for him, the veil was gossamer.

Two years later, I huddled under the quilts and sobbed loudly, not caring who heard. The man I had married in the Salt Lake Temple had left our family and left the Church, and I felt abandoned. Despondent. Shoved out of my comfort zone, far from the things that could bring me peace.

Far from them, that is, until fifteen-year-old Nicholas tentatively opened the door, crept to my bed, and crawled in next to me. Putting his arms around me once again, he quietly told me, "Oh, Mom, don't cry. You still have your sacred covenants. You still have the blessing of your relationship with the Lord, and nothing Dad does will ever take that from you."

Suddenly, there it was—the peace I had so desperately needed.

A week before leaving on his mission, Nicholas expressed his desire to do the temple work for his brother, who had died just before turning twenty-one. A week after receiving his own endowment, Nicholas and I entered the Mount Timpanogos Temple for that hallowed purpose. I waited patiently in the chapel while Nicholas acted as proxy, receiving the Melchizedek Priesthood and completing the initiatory on behalf of his brother.

I will never forget the feelings that washed over my soul as he sat next to me in the chapel. He literally beamed; heaven was near. Leaning close to my ear, he whispered, "Mom, Daniel's here. He's *here*."

There have been so many other sublime experiences—times I knew beyond any doubt that Nicholas does, indeed, have a testimony of the Savior. That his birth mother's great desire was born of inspiration, that our Father knew this was a singular spirit who had much to accomplish and many souls to bless.

Those two failed attempts to adopt a baby were painful. Confusing. Frustrating. Difficult to reconcile. But they were necessary steps in a process that led to some of the greatest joy I have ever known. That joy did not come from the baby I held in my arms. That joy, ultimately, came in my readiness to allow my will to be swallowed up in God's.

My joy did not come because I finally got what I wanted. My joy emanated from a deeper, more quenching relationship with a Father who holds each of us in the hollow of His hand—who loves us more than we can comprehend, who has designed for each of us individually a plan that will enable us to experience immeasurable joy and peace here and hereafter.

In the end, my joy came from better understanding my Heavenly Father. From developing the patience to place on the altar the only thing that is truly mine to give: my will. From at last grasping—truly recognizing—that to trust Him is to trust His timing. To know that all of those things—surrendering my will to His, patiently waiting for *His* due time—lead along the only sure path to joy.

The words of Elder Joseph B. Wirthlin, delivered in his Sunday morning address of the October 2006 general conference in which he referred to the Resurrection, testify to me of the joy that awaits each of us as we trust with faith: "Each of us will have our own Fridays—those days when the universe itself seems shattered and the shards of our world lie littered about us in pieces. We all will experience those broken times when it seems we can never be put together again. We will all have our Fridays. But I testify to you in the name of the One who conquered death—Sunday will come. In the darkness of our sorrow, Sunday will come. No matter our desperation, no matter our grief, Sunday will come. In this life or the next, Sunday will come."[11]

That Friday found the Savior of all mankind facing a trial incomprehensible to us, the most difficult thing anyone has been asked to do. It found Him pushing deeper into the Garden, falling on His face in agony, and saying as He faced that most horrifying ordeal, "O my Father, if it be possible, let this cup pass from me: *nevertheless not as I will, but as thou wilt.*"[12] It was a Friday more terrible than any of us will ever be asked to face.

Yet it led to a Sunday that was the most magnificent of any ever experienced. For on that brilliant Sunday morn, the angels told those astonished disciples who sought their Master, "He is not here: for he is risen, as he said."[13] Risen so that all of us might also rise. Risen because the will of the ever-obedient Son was swallowed up in the will of the Father. Risen to give every one of us life everlasting.

There can be no greater joy.

---

11 "Sunday Will Come," *Ensign*, Nov. 2006.

12 Matthew 26:39; emphasis added.

13 Matthew 28:6.

I had my Fridays, but once I committed to His will and forgot my own, my Sunday came, yielding a greater gift than I ever could have imagined.

My Sunday came, and so will yours. Despite all the Fridays, so will yours.

PART II: MARRIAGE

Chapter 3
Joy in Unanswered Prayers: An Update Story
By Laryssa Waldron

A Holding Pattern

"Ladies and Gentlemen, this is your captain speaking. We have not been given clearance to land at Salt Lake International yet; hoping to do that soon, but in the meantime, we will be in a holding pattern and ask that you sit tight for a moment."

I have faced my own holding pattern for over a decade. Almost a decade and a half. I know many of us have had longer ones, many shorter, but whatever the wait, it can be a frustrating time—and yet, one in which a lot can be learned.

A large factor in my holding pattern is that my husband is bipolar.

Sometimes that sentence evokes emotion, and if you have had experience with mental illness you understand the weight I carry when I write that sentence. Please understand that he is a good man but has a very difficult illness that has had a tremendous effect on our lives over the course of our fifteen-year marriage. We have tried to live as close to the traditional family model (husband working while mom stays home) as possible while raising our young children, both for personal and spiritual reasons. In 2007, we temporarily moved into my parents' basement apartment to help our situation. Ten years later, we were still there.

We faced many trials in the safety of that space. (I will not chronicle the tedious soap opera of illness, job changes and losses, health issues, and selfish and stupid decisions we both made over the last many years—just know that life has been difficult.) Amidst it all, God's compensatory nature helped us gain beautiful blessings and opportunities. But every time I thought I'd be able to get out of the holding pattern, I kept being put back in by necessity, consequences, or personal revelation.

GUILT AND JOY

My life consisted of being the caretaker to my broken-down, sick husband as well as my three darling daughters. I was the safe space, the place to land, and the person who built and patched them up and got them ready to face another day. If I couldn't help, I taught them how to get help and strength from God. I was the nurturer. I was Eve, the mother of those living in that little basement apartment.

All the while, God was my caretaker, patching me up and giving me strength to face another day. However, all of the no's, the weight of constantly living in a state of poverty, and the endless cycles of illness, job loss, and disappointment began to take a toll on my spirit. Often, I felt overwhelmed by guilt, staying as a mother in the home, only working part-time while my broken, sick husband and my broken, sick parents worked. Many people thought I was crazy and even selfish. I often wondered about this; how can we get joy when we are not doing what the world around us thinks is the best course for our lives?

But the truth is every time—without exception—I took my concerns to the Lord, I was told to stay. For years and years, He told me to stay doing what I was doing—difficult, yes, but I knew the course of my life was acceptable to God and, moreover, that it was His will. President N. Eldon Tanner put it best when he said, "How much more satisfying it is when we receive the praise of God, knowing that it is fully justified and that his love and respect for us will persist, when usually the praise of men is fleeting and most disappointing."[14]

God's will was evident by the long list of brilliant ideas, schemes, and job opportunities I would try and fail at. Every time Bryan faced a difficulty, I would apply for a full-time job, but then I wouldn't get it, and I would be reassured again that, in staying home, I was doing what was right for my family. So, despite the sometimes soul-destroying difficulties, I chose to be obedient and wait on the Lord.

AN INTENSE PRAYER AND A POLICY CHANGE

In the fall of 2014, I poured my heart out to the Lord, aching because I missed the companionship He and I had before I was married, when I was a single seminary teacher. That's not to say that one can't be close to God without being a seminary teacher, but for me, my identity, my joy . . . I

---

14 "For They Loved the Praise of Men More Than the Praise of God." *Ensign*. Oct. 1975.

always felt whole when teaching in a religious classroom. And I missed that closeness. I told Him in prayer that if my life was truly to be an endless cycle of looping that led me back to my basement home *for-ev-er*, I was okay with that, but something, anything, had to change to make things a little bit better! Something had to be a "yes," something had to work out, because the circles were making me a little bit crazy (and threatening to destroy the little Pollyanna in my soul).

Please, I begged Him, *send something to help me!*

Two weeks later, a policy changed that opened the door for me to potentially be a seminary teacher again. It would call for an intense seminary teacher training program I'd have to start from scratch, as if I had never done it before, and a grueling year-and-a-half bid to try to get hired—with no thought to the years of previous seven years' experience I'd had in that job. I had *amazing* family support to help with my youngest child, Ruby, who was a year old, and spiritual help from on high to hold down two part-time jobs (student teaching two seminary classes and a class at Salt Lake Community College as an English adjunct professor), do lesson preps, hold a demanding Church calling, and continue to be the wife and mother at home.

It was a struggle, but I was nourished spiritually so deeply that I felt more alive than I had for a very long time. It was like drinking directly from a fire hydrant and filling up reserves of water that had been severely depleted.

Spring of 2016

Toward the end of my student teaching, I began having problems in my classes. Things that were previously going well seemed to unravel, and always, it occurred when someone was there to evaluate my class. I felt like I kept missing at the free throw line. I asked for a blessing, and in a prayer before the blessing, I explained that I needed to make some baskets soon if I was to be hired. In the blessing, I was told that my bid for full-time employment would be successful, and then I received some blessings and cautions about my future as a working mother. Then I was told to hand the ball to the Lord and let Him take the shot.

I did. I gave everything I had to Him, and in April 2016, I was told I would not be rehired.

It was crushing.

It was painful and heart-wrenching, not only because it was a huge disappointment, but also because my family needed it for our physical survival.

I understood what camaraderie I was being denied. I had friends who had been hired at the same time I had been who were now at levels I had hoped to one day achieve by my current age. Certainly, had I not followed the promptings of the Spirit, I would be a success in my forties. But then again, would I have been? If I had not followed the promptings of the Holy Ghost, would I have been able to be successful in life? It hurt my brain to think about it.

SLCC and Moving Forward

In May, I finished my semester at SLCC and was down to only one part-time job, which was also winding down, and in my free time, I took my little two-year-old to the zoo. I marveled at how wonderful it was to look at the world through the eyes of my beautiful baby and how much I had missed that year.

Because I hadn't arranged for classes that summer at SLCC, I had no job. And we were poor. And again (but this time it was my fault), we made the exhausting rounds for help to financially and physically survive as my poor husband fought through his mental illness and tried to support our family alone.

The guilt set in, along with the frustrations and the demons—demons that told me to "curse God and die."15 The demons that told me I was worthless. The demons that told me to be bitter and blame those who didn't rehire me.

The problem was that I loved God too much to curse, leave, or forsake Him. Our relationship—all the help, experiences, and prayers both answered and unanswered—was very real. It was like making a candle. For over forty years, I'd been dipping the candle and letting the wax cool, making a larger and larger stick with every experience we'd had together. By this point in my life, it was so large that I didn't have the luxury of saying the candle didn't exist, like my atheist friends. No, I couldn't turn from Him now. I continued in my relationship, treating God like a dear family member, working it out, continuing in our friendship. And because of my relationship with Him, I learned to not believe the demons that said I was worthless. And because I was trying to be like Him, I spent the summer putting the names of those who didn't rehire me on the temple prayer roll and in my personal prayers while I forged ahead.

The world would blame me for not jumping into a full-time teaching job years ago at the first sign of problems or for not leaving my husband. But I didn't. I followed the promptings of the Spirit for my life.

15 Job 2:9.

But now the floodgates were open. How could I ever teach anything else now that I had tasted teaching religion again after so many years? I missed how it filled my soul, and I missed the person I was when the Lord and I worked together in the classroom, now even more than I had previously!

I began to search for other teaching opportunities and found that BYU-Idaho was hiring a full-time professor of religion for the next year. I jokingly asked Bryan if he wanted to move to Rexburg, and he said, "Sure!" so I applied. On the day that the applications closed, I got a rejection letter.

In the fall of 2016, I took on three courses of the new English program at SLCC, which, because of the new guidelines, demanded more of my time and paid little in terms of my soul. Imagine teaching a course in which you required the students to write about the problems of the world, and yet you didn't have the ability to teach the one solution, the one Being who could give the aching heart peace and all the justice and mercy needed in a dark and painful world! Without the Savior, there can never be justice for the countless lives full of pain that have existed on this earth. Our society can never right those wrongs. There is no other ideology, teaching, or religion that promises *complete* restoration, peace, mercy, and equity. "And God shall wipe away all tears from their eyes; and there shall be no more death, neither sorrow, nor crying, neither shall there be any more pain: for the former things are passed away."[16]

Teaching in that circumstance felt like trying to paint without my hands. One night, I read and discussed four papers—three on horrific child abuse and one on the life of a serial killer and how he came to commit those heinous crimes. How could there be any justice for those children whose lives had been shattered, for those who had been tortured and murdered, without a Savior? There was no promise without Him, no way that our society could give back what was taken from those souls with any social advocacy. My heart broke and my soul was heavy because I was not allowed to feed the students. By January 2017, I was exhausted and in a deep funk as I faced another semester of the same work and my husband, who had again changed jobs, began to be disenchanted by his new one. We were back in the same holding pattern. I didn't want to even face life—the basic care of self and family.

An Unexpected Twist

Then the unimaginable happened. In February, I got a phone call from BYU-Idaho, and I was invited to interview for a three-year visiting position

16 Revelation 21:4.

as a professor of religion while a brother served as a mission president. I had been recommended by an amazing seminary principal, Heidi Weed, with whom I had worked while doing my student teaching the year before. It would only be temporary, so they worried about me bringing my family to Rexburg under those circumstances. I credited them for their kind concerns, but honestly, how could I explain to them my situation that spanned the last years without having them taste the desperation I felt? Since we had never been settled as a family, I simply assured them that we would be fine and that we understood the risks involved.

All I wanted to do when I went up to the interview was not seem as pathetic and broken down as I felt. I begged the Lord to be with me during my teaching experience, to allow His Spirit to teach the students in class that day so I wouldn't waste their time with another lesson that was for me about trying and failing. I just didn't want to miss, even though I felt sure that the other teacher who was there would be chosen for the job above me. Given my track record over the past twelve years and the fact that they wanted someone who could easily go back to their old job after the three years was over, I just wanted to feel like I was a strong competitor. It was a very beautiful, sacred experience being in the classroom that day, a lovely memory. And then I had to wait until April to hear the final choice.

Which was the other teacher.

But . . .

ALLOWED TO LAND

I was told in a dream a few weeks before that I wasn't going to get the job but that there was another position. And in the same phone call that told me that I wasn't going to get the job, I was told there was still a possibility I would get hired.

Three days later, I was on the way to the temple. I was grieving for some different friends who had been hit with tragic news. Three separate friends and three separate circumstances, all very difficult, and I was carrying them in my heart and in my prayers that day. As I got to the corner near the temple, I noticed a homeless woman who was selling some beaded bracelets she had made. I went to speak to her because I thought it was neat, and we discussed her circumstances, how hard life was, what we did in the temple, and how she had been making more money with the bracelets than she had begging. My phone rang, and though I had already put it on vibrate and was about to ignore it, I got an impression to check it. I excused myself. It was an Idaho number.

I answered and was invited to take a three-year teaching position as a professor of religion at BYU-Idaho. I was cleared for landing. But what a job! It was even more than I could have ever dreamed of and exactly what I had hoped to achieve with my professional career all those years ago as a young, new seminary teacher.

But as I looked over at the homeless woman and thought of all my suffering friends, I remembered that I had been only a step away from homelessness myself, and I had gone through some truly difficult trials as well. God's billions of children would all be in and out of hard things and holding patterns. Over the years, I had been tutored by God in some intense life lessons of mortality—disease, poverty, humility, sacrifice, agency, and trust. I had come to believe that the mysteries of godliness were not about the dinosaurs and Kolob, but about learning to be like God in the mortal condition. The questions of life became even more real. How can we live when others' choices cause us intense physical and mental pain and anguish? How do we stay silent like the Savior did while those around us are spitting false accusations about our character? How do we forgive someone who has wounded us? How do we keep reaching out in prayer when the heavens are silent? How do we have faith when we can't see the promised blessings? How do we love God when He's stripping us down to absolute nothingness and then, without a breather, adds another layer of trial? How do we serve another while we are going through our own agonizing circumstances? All of these the Savior experienced and overcame as He faced His final few hours on earth. All of this is what the divine tutoring of mortality is about, to become like the Savior.

"Beloved, think it not strange concerning the fiery trial which is to try you, as though some strange thing happened unto you: But rejoice, inasmuch as ye are partakers of Christ's sufferings; that, when his glory shall be revealed, ye may be glad also with exceeding joy."[17]

If we do not learn the lessons of mortality and the mysteries of godliness, what a waste this earth life experience will be!

So, I praised God in the temple and thanked Him in deep humility for this opportunity. I also prayed fervently for my friends to endure their difficulties well.

When I finished in the temple, I went to the bank to withdraw money from the little bit we had, and I bought a pink-pearl beaded bracelet from the homeless woman to remind me that life is so very fragile, and I invited her to come to church so that she too could go to the temple someday.

---

17 1 Peter 4:12–13.

REXBURG, IDAHO

I sit here in a phenomenally beautiful rental home, having finished my first full year of my three-year teaching contract. Working daily hand in hand with the holy Spirit in the classroom and testifying of the Savior and His Atonement has been a joyous, marvelous, and sacred experience. I am in awe of the students, the faculty, and the staff here; BYU–I is a very special place. My heart is daily drawn out in great gratitude for this teaching gift; it is a true miracle.

My husband got a job at the college as well, and it has been a blessing to work together. We go on lunch dates and to devotionals together, which gives added strength to our relationship.

Working full-time, being a wife and mom, and running a household has been quite a juggle, but my little family and I have been trained for this in previous circumstances. Everyone pitches in to help. There is still an uncertain future, with trials to face and worries ahead, but God is good.

My secret to joy in this life, come whatever the future holds, is my relationship with the Lord. Nephi tells us that the tree of life is the love of God. It is freely given to all who live on this earth and can be felt in their hearts. That love comes from the Savior, the Lamb of God, the Son of the Eternal Father, and that love is the most desirable above all things and the most joyous to the soul.[18] We can choose to have that love, companionship, and joy in our lives for fleeting moments, or we can choose to have it for longer periods of time, depending on our actions.

When the Lord doesn't answer, leaves a confusing message, or puts me in a holding pattern, I have come to view those moments as I would in any relationship—I imagine that He's in a meeting, and I have to leave a message on the answering machine. So, I pray and leave a message, knowing He'll get it and answer me when He chooses to call me back. You see, just because He doesn't answer me once in a while doesn't mean our friendship is over. I still reach out. I am in a covenant relationship with Him. It does not end when the fire gets hot. For me, it does not end at all. My great joy is that as a God of truth, when He says it does not end for Him either, it won't. Security and stability in this life are fragile, but God is everlasting. He is my eternal friend and yours.

It's been quite a journey, and I wish you all the best on yours. God is a giver of good gifts; it's just that sometimes the right opportunities have to

---

18 See 1 Nephi 11:21–23.

work themselves out. Some of the airplanes below us have to move out of the way. This mortal probation is a test, and if we endure triumphantly, there will be rich blessings both now and in the life to come. I know that as we befriend or continue to deepen our relationship with the Savior, we will have our own future happy landings as well—we will find eternal joy.[19]

---

19 See Laryssa's original story in *I Can Do Hard Things with God*, by Ganel-Lyn Condie, chpt. 13.

Chapter 4
Finding Joy, Finding Each Other:
An Update Story

By Betsy and Darin Eckton

BETSY

MANY YEARS AGO, A FRIEND shared with me the results of a research study that concluded that the happiest people were those who were happily married. The next happiest group was those who were happily single. Following those were the unhappily single, and last in happiness was the group who were unhappily married. I did not know how this research study defined happiness or what methods had been employed in reaching these findings, but I reflected on the stated conclusions. As a single person whose desire to be married had not yet been fulfilled, I determined to live as happily as possible. I fully trusted in my loving Heavenly Father, who had a true and eternal personal plan of happiness for me, and I knew His plan for me was perfect and would bring greater joy to my life than any plan I had for myself—although, of course, in my own opinion, my plans for myself were exceptional.

So how does one find maximum joy when not yet living what is identified as the ideal? I believe that although it happened subconsciously, I began to wrestle with the related concepts of joy, happiness, and fun. There were many around me whom I observed seeking fun, but that "fun" did not always lead to happiness, and some fun had no chance of leading to joy. I too enjoyed fun and took great pleasure in traveling, attending the theater, making trips to Disneyland, scuba diving, and participating in other activities with family and good friends.

I knew I would not be happy if I didn't have meaningful and fulfilling employment and financial security, so I made investments, worked to improve my skills and advance my career, and sought opportunities to further my education, eventually earning my doctoral degree.

But beyond fun and happiness, I found true and lasting joy as I sought opportunities to learn and grow in meaningful ways. Joy came as I served in the temple and in my Church callings, as I engaged in personal gospel study, and as I worked to become what I felt my Father in Heaven wished me to become. In short, I believe the great joy in my life has always come from living my covenants.

Yet the opportunity to receive the greatest joy by kneeling at a sacred altar and making the blessed covenant of eternal marriage eluded me. And perhaps, at least to a certain degree, when the Lord began to open that door, I eluded it.

DARIN

I grew up playing multiple competitive sports and gave little attention to dating, though most of my close friends were girls. I was a boy who longed for companionship yet feared going out of my comfort zone and especially feared rejection in the dating scene. Almost as if I had blinders on, I set aside several offers to play soccer and/or baseball at the collegiate level and chose a path familiar to many as I enrolled at Brigham Young University. I did not go to BYU thinking I would serve a mission, though the Lord knew I would gain the preparatory experiences I needed to strengthen my testimony and gain a commitment to serve Him.

When I returned from my mission in Argentina, I resumed my studies at BYU, and I also started working as a teacher at the Missionary Training Center. I knew getting married was the proverbial next step, so it was something I desired, but I did not actively pursue it. I started hanging out with a girl who regularly expressed her desire to have a family lifestyle consistent with what I had experienced in my home, which was very attractive. We were engaged within about a month and then married in the temple. We were blessed with six amazing children (five alive and one in heaven). Most of our married life, I was in school, working on my master's and doctorate degrees while also working full-time at BYU. I was blessed with several wonderful opportunities to serve in the Church as well. In fact, it was while I was serving as a counselor in the stake presidency that my marriage ended.

To say that I was devastated is an understatement! In my mind, my storybook eternal family was now ending. How could this happen? In my grief, I wanted my life to end. I didn't feel like my life had any value. This experience brought me to my knees both figuratively and literally. I remembered Elder

D. Todd Christofferson's talk "As Many As I Love, I Rebuke and Chasten." I had one of two choices to make: 1) I could either allow my pain and grief to consume me, to allow the fears of what people might think of me, my failures, my shortcomings, and every other negative thought and feeling I was experiencing to define me, or 2) I could truly apply the principles I had known in my mind and had been teaching the members of my stake over the pulpit for many years. I decided to look to the Lord as Enos did, and I "cried unto him in mighty prayer and supplication for mine own soul; and all the day long did I cry unto him; yea, and when the night came I did still raise my voice high that it reached the heavens."[20] This Enos-like wrestle was my daily experience for weeks and even months. The Lord was extending a very personal and loving invitation to come unto Him and become converted, not just in my mind but deep in my heart.

Fulfilling my covenant relationships became even more paramount. I began to worship in the temple weekly, to engage more deeply in my relationship with my Savior. Every two weeks, I began calling all the temples in Utah and placing the names of my family on the prayer rolls because I knew I needed all the faith and strength I could get. Some days were more difficult than others, and I had to press forward through a sustained period of depression. However, as the days, weeks, and months passed, I began to see myself more clearly than I ever had before. I knew I was a son of a God who loved me, and I loved Him in a very intimate and personal covenant relationship. In His tender mercies, He helped me see that even though my marital relationship was ending, I did not have to choose to let this experience define my identity or worth. Possibly similar to Enos, the Lord's voice validated me, reassuring me that my sins were forgiven ahead of the difficult task ahead, that I would be blessed, and that my guilt and fears were swept away. Like the people of the Americas who Christ healed and made whole, I felt His healing power; He was making me whole.

As Enos turned his heart to the welfare of his brethren, I turned my heart and efforts even more completely to the welfare of my children—"Wherefore, I did pour out my whole soul unto God for them."[21] I was blessed with a very clear revelation wherein God told me, "They were mine before they were yours. They are still mine." In His omniscient mercy, even a couple years before the divorce, the Lord blessed me with my job as a professor. With this job came significant flexibility with my time and allowed me to continue to

20 Enos 1:4.
21 Enos 1:9.

support my children in their school and other activities, as I had previously done—although now in a shared-custody arrangement.

Betsy

Unbeknownst to me, a dear friend had received a prompting nearly twenty years previously that she would one day set me up with someone significant. She kept this bit of personal revelation to herself, at times expressing some reluctance to the Lord for what she felt was a responsibility she was willing to forego. However, for nearly two decades, she periodically revisited this prompting and faithfully considered possibilities.

I was excited for her when she decided to return to school and pursue her long-awaited university degree through online courses at Brigham Young University—Idaho. Two weeks into a new semester, she received a very clear prompting that her online professor was the individual she was supposed to introduce me to. Given this potentially awkward situation, she continued to keep both the earlier and latter promptings to herself until after the semester ended.

The promptings continued, and on the night of her daughter's wedding reception, she knew she had to say something to me. As we visited after the reception, without mentioning any of the promptings, she broached the subject of a possible set-up with her professor. I balked. The timing was challenging. I was in the middle of completing my dissertation, writing in thirty-hour stints without sleep, and could see no feasible way that I could make time for a date. My poor friend was thwarted as she tried to follow the will of the Lord! So what did she do? What any loyal friend and obedient servant of the Lord would do. She went behind my back.

Darin

After my divorce, I remained a member of my stake but moved into another ward through the kind and very generous offer of friends to occupy their basement for as long as my kids and I needed. I enjoyed teaching the Gospel Doctrine class. I was moving forward with my journey in life. Yet, as I longed for eternal companionship, I began to pray to God for guidance and began discussing with the Lord the kinds of attributes and characteristics I needed for my own growth, for the growth of my children, and for a person with whom I would be equally yoked and could share the eternities. I never felt compelled to enter the world of online dating, and I went to one single adult activity, mostly to encourage a friend to go, and that did not appeal to me. I began to tell the Lord I would like to find my eternal companion but asked for His forgiveness because I was using "workless" faith. I wasn't doing all I could,[22] but in the end, I knew He knew my heart and my commitment to Him.

There were several wonderful single sisters in my ward and within the stake whom I knew and loved. In fact, I attempted to set up a date with one of them through a series of anonymous creative messages that I left her in a variety of places over a period of a couple weeks, including her place of employment—BYU—that were intended to culminate in a meeting. That attempt at dating ended in her asking a BYU police officer to give me a letter she'd written and an invitation from the kind officer to cease any and all contact with her. After that experience, the talk "Wrong Roads," from Elder Jeffrey R. Holland came to mind, where he said, "There are times when the only way to get from A to C is by way of B." Paraphrasing Elder Holland, God's wish is to get us on the right road as quickly as possible with as much reassurance as we need. Sometimes the easiest way to do this is to allow us to go only a short distance down the wrong road and know very quickly, without a doubt, that it is the wrong road. At least for me, this dating road I'd taken was a humorous wrong road.

Well, I was a little deflated after being rejected using my creative romanticism to pursue my first post-divorce date. I decided I wouldn't worry about trying to date, yet I continued praying for a miracle to find somebody (yet again, workless faith, which I don't usually recommend, but in this case, I can see the Lord was giving me very small reassurances that my expressions of workless faith were not falling on deaf ears).

Then it happened. I received an email from an online student who had just taken a class from me. It was the summer of 2015. In this email, the student asked if I would be interested in being set up on a date. Believe me, there were many, many friends, ward and stake members, current and former students, and others who had asked me if they could set me up. Because I had to prioritize my time very carefully, especially spending all the time I could with my kids, I asked the Lord to inspire me to know which relationships I should pursue. I had never felt inspired to pursue any of these very kind offers to set me up on a date until this one. I trusted this person, though she was just the vehicle who was simply acting on her own divine revelation. In reality, the Lord blessed both of us to act.

22 See 2 Nephi 25:23.

After expressing interest in the set-up, I did not hear from her for several days. When she did contact me, she sent me a very lengthy email with pictures of Betsy, some of Betsy's many accomplishments, including being awarded Utah Valley 2014 Mother to the Community as a single woman, stories of her international humanitarian service, and a reassurance of Betsy's commitment to her covenants.

As I read this email, in my mind, I surprisingly said, "Check. Check. Check. And check." The Spirit was reminding me that what I was reading aligned exactly with the characteristics and attributes of the type of person I had been describing to my Heavenly Father in my prayers. After reading this miraculous description of what sounded like a perfect woman for me, I immediately felt impressed to ask my two oldest daughters to read the email and share their reactions to the idea of my pursuing a date with somebody like this.

They both said, "She sounds amazing! Are you going to ask her out?"

I then said, "I think so."

I was extremely nervous to call her. In fact, I dialed her number and then hung up before the phone began to ring. I dialed again, and her phone rang and rang and eventually went to voice mail, which was probably a tender mercy to calm my nerves and allow me to leave a message and place the ball in her court.

Betsy

The first voice mail I received was indecipherable. The sound was so garbled I could make out only a word or two. But the number was on caller ID, so I returned the call, leaving a voice mail of my own. A short game of phone tag later, we finally spoke in a seemingly brief conversation that lasted about one and a half hours. Given the challenging nature of both our schedules, the only time we could find to meet was on a Monday night at nine-fifteen. We decided to cook dinner together at my home.

The soup was delicious, but it was the natural conversation and ease of working together that struck me.

Darin

The moment I stepped inside the door of her house, I felt the Spirit of God, and it all felt very familiar. In fact, the words, "This is very familiar. I could live here," came into my mind.

BETSY

We sat at the table and ate and talked for another three or four hours. During that time, I had a very clear witness from the Spirit that this was the person I was going to marry. Not only did I have that witness, but the Spirit also confirmed to my heart and mind that he knew it too. What do you do with that kind of direct communication from the heavens? In the moment, nothing but wait in wonder. It was likely that the God of heaven and earth, in His great omniscience, understood that the girl who couldn't even order decisively at a restaurant would need a good kick upside the head if she were to make a commitment of a much more eternal nature. However, it was the peace that accompanied that revelation and continued unwaveringly that carried me through.

DARIN

We spent as much time together as we could that week. One day I was with my two oldest daughters, the two who had asked if I was going to ask Betsy out, and we ended up going to visit Betsy so they could meet her.

They enjoyed her and her home, and one daughter even volunteered to spend time helping Betsy that Saturday in her costume room for about six hours. The following week was Thanksgiving break, and I had already made plans to visit my parents and other family in Washington State, which also happened to be where much of Betsy's family lived, so we didn't spend time together that week. Yet, I found myself texting and emailing with Betsy multiple times each day while we were apart. We would send each other photos, updates, and many other tidbits. I wanted to share everything with her. As I described her to my parents, I told them she was a woman with whom I felt I could share the eternities.

My father said she sounded like a remarkable woman, kind of like his stepmother was for him and his father.

Betsy offered to pick me up from the airport in Salt Lake City, and she took me to dinner as a way to "return the favor" for the dinner we made on our first date. We picked up right where we had left off, and again, everything was natural and effortless. The Lord truly blessed us to know quickly that we were meant to be with each other, to continue learning and growing together, to love, and to enjoy the journey of life together. Not too much more time passed before we openly declared our feelings, including sharing the promptings we had had about marriage and the eternities. It was nice to be self-aware and secure enough to feel like we could be open with each other so early in our relationship.

I was struck with awe at the great goodness of my Father in Heaven. I was in my midforties and had pretty much resigned myself to the idea that the Lord's plan for me did not include marriage in this lifetime. But here He had presented me with someone who was seemingly the perfect match for me. Darin had all the qualities I had told my Father in Heaven I wanted in a husband and many traits even beyond what I might have hoped for. His dedication to the Lord, to his covenants, and to service was evident, and we openly discussed spiritual goals. His commitment to his children and his amazing way of interacting with them clearly demonstrated to me that he was the type of father I wanted my children to have. His work ethic was obvious, and I was impressed by his ability to accomplish so much each day. I admired his strong intelligence and fun-loving sense of humor. I loved that he was passionate about family history and humanitarian service and so many other shared interests and ideals. And he was kind, patient, attentive, and loving. I enjoyed talking with him, laughing with him, and even sharing tears with him as we expressed the deeper sentiments of our hearts. Our life experiences evidenced to each other who we were and who we wanted to be, and it was clear that we could readily join hands in a shared journey. It was all so natural, so effortless, and so very beautiful.

Why does a single person purchase a 4,800 sq. ft., six-bedroom home? So that seven years later, in March 2016, upon being sealed in the Payson Utah Temple, I could welcome a husband and five beautiful children into that home.

Going from a household of one to a household of seven has presented challenges. As our first anniversary approached, many people asked what I had learned during that year. The answer was easy—I had learned about my many faults. I knew about and had been consistently working to overcome my faults for endless years, but nothing had ever brought an awareness of my failings and inadequacies as instant wife and motherhood had. My prayers intensified, and I worked each day to be a little better than the day before. It is a daily path I continue to walk.

Indeed, nearly every aspect of my life changed. I no longer had sole control over my schedule, the car, what was for dinner, or most other facets of day-to-day living. Challenging? Yes! Filled with joy? Oh yes!

Nothing can compare with the joy of a heart filled with love. And just when I believe that I can't love my family any more than I do, I find my heart growing so that sometimes I feel it might burst from so much love. Walking hand in hand with a husband with whom I can share my hopes and dreams, my sorrows, and my heartaches and in whom I can trust to help me learn and grow is a tremendous source of joy.

DARIN & BETSY

Our covenant relationship blesses us with joy each day. In his general conference address of April 2006, President Russell M. Nelson said, "Marriage brings greater possibilities for happiness than does any other human relationship," and we have felt these possibilities come to fruition in our lives. We have the privilege of being parents to five living children and strive to help them look to the Savior and their Heavenly Father and to make and keep their covenants in everything we do. As do all families, we face many challenges, some of them quite serious, and we make many mistakes in the process. Each day, we press forward again with faith in a loving Father in Heaven and His Son, Jesus Christ.

In all this learning and growth, we have much joy . . . and happiness . . . and fun. We intentionally strive to devote time to family games, movie nights, road trips, and backyard campouts. We seek to give of ourselves and have had the privilege of serving in our local ward and neighborhood, as well as leading students in humanitarian service in Ghana, Peru, and Nepal. We attend our children's dance and cheer competitions, choir concerts, swim meets, and science fairs.

We openly acknowledge and emphasize that the experiences we describe represent our own unique individual and collective journeys. Each individual journey might share some similarities or none at all. Regardless of the situation, we hope our story provides personal insights and principles that are helpful, meaningful, and instructive to each of us as a child of a loving Heavenly Father. Most importantly, we hope each reader will receive what God wants to teach them through His Holy Spirit. Each of us has our own unique journey in mortality that allows us to choose and to change, to become more like our Savior and His loving Father. He wants each of us, as His child, to become like Him and to return to His presence. He wants our happiness in this life and in the eternities. In His omniscient and merciful way of considering our moral agency to act, He does all He can to bring about His work and His glory. As such, sometimes our journey in mortality takes unexpected turns, U-turns, and side streets, but all things work together for our good as we strive to find joy in living our covenants, as promised in Doctrine and Covenants 90:24.[23]

---

23 See the Ecktons' original story in *I Can Do Hard Things with God*, by Ganel-Lyn Condie, chpt. 14.

Part III: HEALTH

Chapter 5
The Elusiveness of Joy: My Journey with Chronic Suffering
By Anita Stansfield

I AM A NOVELIST BY trade; I write bedtime stories for grown-ups. My instinct, as well as my training, have taught me that it's impossible for a reader to appreciate the important moral of a story if they aren't shown the conflict and important details that lead to that ever-important happy ending. And I do believe in happy endings, even if we have to wait until the next life to receive the blessings we are working toward.

This story is about the search for my own happy ending and the surprisingly difficult journey I was required to take in that search.

Nobody stands at the threshold of their earliest memories and thinks or even believes that they are going to have a difficult life. It's not a goal anyone sets or a path any sane person seeks out. What we instinctively seek for is happiness; we want life to be enjoyable and free of stress and challenge.

This was certainly true for me. But I've learned there is a certain obliviousness that comes with the way being too easy. And though we prefer to be carefree, would we choose to be so unaware of what matters most?

Like any other child, I grew up with no awareness of the dysfunctional behaviors going on around me in my home. I hold a great reverence and respect for my parents; they were good people doing the best they knew how. They loved us and made certain our every need and comfort was provided. They sincerely wanted their children to be happy. But they didn't live in a day when such things as proactive parenting were even understood, much less acknowledged or discussed publicly. They did the best they could with what they had, and they made many noble sacrifices for which I will always be grateful. However, the journey of my adult life has uncovered—little by little—how damaged I was when I emerged into adulthood and how that damage impacted every facet of my life. But it wasn't until I was sinking in the quicksand of physical and emotional suffering that my years of trying to learn the answers of my own life and come to terms with them finally began to come together, and it became increasingly evident that I had so much more to learn.

For years, I was a person who instinctively wanted to do the right thing, who believed God would hear and answer my prayers, and who wanted to please Him because I needed Him on my side. It wasn't until my midtwenties that I began to doubt the way of thinking and believing that had gotten me to that point. When my life as a wife and young mother clashed boldly with the screaming need inside of me to be a novelist, I realized I had always *believed* in the religious teachings of my childhood, but I needed to *know*. I had to know for myself that these things were indeed true, or I would never be able to continue on paths I believed were right but were proving to be so difficult.

With time, study, heart-wrenching prayer, and much pondering, I was finally blessed with an absolute, undeniable answer—but I didn't know how difficult following through on that answer would become or how the difficulty would only increase over the years. My commitment became firm and solid to live my religion, remain devoted to my family . . . and write and share with the world the stories that haunted me continually, like some kind of schizophrenic voice in my brain that refused to be still. I absolutely knew I needed to write, and I would somehow be able to do so and still be a good wife and mother.

Years passed, more children came into our family, and I trudged along day by day, week by week, serving in the Church, caring for my home and family, and writing every minute I could possibly manage, while simultaneously collecting rejection letters from publishers and agents that were discouraging and disheartening, but they did nothing to halt my determination to become a published novelist, to be able to share my stories with readers who could be both entertained and blessed by my books. There were a handful of times I came to the cusp of giving up, but instinctively, I knew my gift of storytelling came from God, and I couldn't quit without knowing He approved. So each time, I fasted and prayed and waited for an answer. Eventually, the answer always came—sometimes in undeniably miraculous ways—and I knew I had to keep writing, even if I didn't understand why. But the journey was never easy, obstacles rose up over and over, and the balancing act of being a good mother and a good writer was a tightrope walk I ventured out on almost every hour for a great many years.

Though I began writing when I was sixteen, I hunkered down and started taking it very seriously—as in writing more than the hours of a full-time job—at the age of twenty-four. My first book was published soon after my thirty-second birthday. My dreams had finally come true, and I had visions of finally having real financial security and being able to have more control over my life and my future—for myself and my family. But I had no idea what trials lay ahead once I became immersed in the publishing industry, nor did I have any inclination that disease was brewing inside me, and my life was on an inevitable downward spiral that would knock me down so thoroughly that every facet of my existence would be strained to its limits.

The month after my first book was released in August 1994, my mother became seriously ill and spent many weeks in the hospital. She died of cancer in January 1998 at the age of seventy. At the time, I had four children, and I knew there was another one who needed to join our family. I didn't know how I could get through pregnancy and childbirth (both of which had previously been very difficult for me) without my mother. But Alyssa was born in June 1999—forced into the world seven weeks early because my blood pressure was threatening to kill me. I now felt complete as a mother, with the arrival of my fifth child, but my health condition was reaching a bursting point.

About the time that we were able to get Alyssa off the cumbersome heart monitor that had been attached to her for seven months, my publishing career (I was up to twelve published books by then) came crashing down around me—all because of a lack of ethics from a few people in powerful positions, which fostered a perfect storm that sent me reeling in my identity as a writer and a woman of faith. And that was when the migraines started. At first I thought it was the combined stress of the difficulty I'd endured from a complicated childbirth and these ugly business matters. But looking back now, I know these things were just contributing factors that started bringing to the surface what had been there for many, many years.

Through the following years, financial struggles became even more challenging, I was raising children in multiple stages of life because my five children were so spread out in age, and my headaches became a frequent companion. I had good days, but I was averaging more than twenty migraines a month, and I started getting chronic muscle pain, along with problems with my neck and hands due to all that writing for so many years without understanding the correct ergonomics of posture and hand placement. Thus began my journey through medical madness.

I lost track of the doctors who would write out a prescription and, when it didn't work, arrogantly dismiss me without making any further attempt to help find the source of the problems. I went through intense physical therapy multiple times that only seemed to make me feel worse. I spent ridiculous amounts of money, invested my deepest hopes, and gradually lost my faith in the medical profession, as well as many alternative healing options. There was no herbal remedy or therapy or medical process that could fix my problems. I was a puzzle and an enigma, and I felt as though I'd been tossed on a trash heap of those who are *unfixable*.

Yet, somehow, through it all, I kept my home under control; even if it was deep with disorder and chaos, it was generally livable and free of germs. I took care of my family and continued to serve in the Church. And I kept writing. I was putting out four books a year but becoming more and more aware that though I was writing for a limited religious market, which was a blessing that helped pay the bills and meet our needs month by month, it was never going to get us out of the debt the many different financial challenges we'd faced over the years had created. Somehow . . . somehow . . . I kept going.

People I worked with in the publishing world called me "the machine" because I could almost magically keep producing novels in spite of my worsening health. It wasn't a title I found flattering in the least, but it certainly seemed appropriate when I realized that when a machine didn't receive proper maintenance, it eventually broke down.

In January 2008, I had an EGD to scope my stomach and upper intestines because I'd begun having terrible stomach aches. I thought I had ulcers. The result was the doctor telling me the lining of my small intestine had the appearance of Celiac Disease. He had taken biopsies and blood, and I would get the results at an appointment in his office the following week.

I was horrified! My mother had had Celiac Disease. I knew what it was and what it meant—or, at least, I knew the version my mother had lived with. In the years since, doctors and scientists had learned more about the disease and how much more serious it was.

During the appointment in which the doctor informed me I had the disease, he explained that I needed to be extremely careful about not ingesting any gluten at all—not even molecules. Celiac is an autoimmune disease triggered by gluten that breaks down the walls of the small intestine so nutrition doesn't get absorbed, and subsequently, the body's systems can start to fail, food allergies can develop, and malnutrition can run rampant.

It can be difficult to diagnose because it has about 250 possible symptoms. Because I hadn't had the same symptoms as my mother, Celiac Disease had never crossed my mind. But when the doctor told me it can cause cancer, a horrifying little light went on in my brain, and I told him my mother, who had had Celiac Disease, had died of cancer. When I answered his questions about the type of cancer and how it had metastasized, he declared with confidence that her cancer had absolutely been caused by the disease. So I walked out of his office reeling, trying to accept that I could never ingest another molecule of gluten and that the disease roiling inside of me was the same one that had killed my mother.

I began furiously researching the disease while I completely changed the structure of my kitchen. Plastic and wood hold molecules of gluten in their pores, even when washed in a dishwasher. Only metals are safe, unless the other utensils are used only for gluten-free foods.

Fun fact: gluten is in almost everything. It's in wheat, rye, and barley, and while most oats are gluten free, they are grown and processed alongside wheat, so oats are not safe unless they are certified gluten free.

Gluten is not required to be declared on a label, and it's hidden in many ingredients. Even "natural flavor" can mean gluten because barley is a common flavoring. It's in dressings and seasonings and beverages, among many other things people wouldn't think of. Going gluten free to this extreme didn't mean removing bread and pasta from my diet. It meant there were very few places I could eat out and be safe, and I could never eat at someone else's home unless I took my own food or gave them strict training on my food preparation. Awkward. It meant I could never be discreet about my disease if I was sharing a meal with other people. It meant never eating the refreshments at any event I attended and never eating at a pot luck. Ever. It meant I couldn't eat sacrament bread, so I had to make special arrangements and have awkward conversations about alternatives—which meant everyone I went to church with knew I was the one who couldn't even tolerate a tiny piece of bread without the threat of being violently ill for weeks or raising my risk of cancer.

My diagnosis was a two-edged sword. I thought that if this was the answer and I could feel better, it would be worth it. At the same time, I became extremely depressed over how dramatically it would change my life—because in this culture, our social lives revolve around food, and I had quickly seen how awkward and challenging it could be. I didn't learn until years later that most of the body's serotonin (the happy hormone) is created in the intestines, which means that depression and anxiety are also common symptoms of Celiac. Well, that explained a lot. Did I mention that I'd always struggled with depression and anxiety? I had just never given myself permission to acknowledge what it was enough to deal with it appropriately.

So, in spite of my depression, I forged ahead, determined to get healthy because I believed that with good health, I could take on the other challenges of my life and handle them. But I didn't get better. I only got worse. I was doing everything my doctors had told me to do, and I had studied and studied to understand my disease and handle it properly. But the headaches continued and the muscle pain and the stomach aches and a growing exhaustion and brain fog that made it difficult to focus.

At the beginning of 2010, I set one goal, and I prayed very hard for God to help me achieve it. I was determined to get healthy once and for all. I asked that I would be guided on a path to better health, and I committed to do whatever it took. The gastroenterologist (digestive system specialist) who had diagnosed me had moved to a different clinic, and my case was given to another doctor; both of these men were reputed as being very good physicians. I trusted my doctor when he dismissed my complaints of ongoing stomach pain as simply being part of the slow healing process of Celiac. Through a strange course of events, I ended up seeing an endocrinologist (hormone specialist), who declared nothing was wrong with my hormones, but she was concerned about a sudden weight gain in my abdomen and ordered an ultrasound. What they found was a horribly diseased gall bladder that needed to be removed ASAP because if a stone moved down the bile duct, it could not only be very painful, but it was also very dangerous.

Late in April 2010, I had my gall bladder removed, and pathology showed it was one of the most diseased gall bladders the surgeon had ever seen. Really? I had two doctors who specialized in the digestive system who had never thought to take a peek at my gall bladder, even given my ongoing complaints of stomach pain? More disillusionment over the medical profession.

Recovery from my surgery was just settling in when I awoke in the middle of the night with such horrible pain in my shoulder that I felt like I'd been shot. It turned out that my fragile neck had finally given out. A disc had slipped and was compressing the nerve cluster that went down my right arm. Of course, it took many weeks, appointments, and ugly tests to make certain this was the case and that surgery could fix it, all the while trying to meet a writing deadline and take care of the requirements of life. I relied heavily on medications and a lot of deep breathing.

When I went to get an MRI of my neck, I also got my annual mammogram, which was a few months past due. They both needed to be done at the same imaging center, and I was able to schedule the appointments back to back. The mammogram looked suspicious, so I had to go back and get another. Really? I remember looking heavenward and saying, "Really?" Deep down, I didn't believe anything was wrong; I just saw it as another distraction, another reason for tests and added misery. But a needle biopsy was scheduled, and that was by far the worst medical procedure I've had done while awake. The biopsy came back as abnormal, but they were vague on what exactly that meant. The doctor advised getting a surgical biopsy in which the tissue of the abnormal area could be removed before it turned into something worse. I wasn't pleased with another surgery, but I certainly wanted to get rid of anything abnormal. However, all my doctors agreed that my neck was far more urgent and that I needed to get that surgery done and regain my strength before I had the surgical biopsy.

At the end of July, I had neck surgery, and ten days later, I was assaulted by a horrible yeast infection, which—jumping ahead—kept happening for a year and half until I got terrible thrush in my mouth. Two doctors later, I finally started treatment for systemic candida. But the neck surgery had apparently been what pushed that over the edge of bursting forth since I'd been given high doses of both antibiotics and steroids in the hospital— both of which kill the healthy bacteria in the body.

In September, the week after I no longer needed a neck brace, my husband was working on replacing the roof of our house. He's good at things like that, and he'd decided to do it himself with a little help from others here and there. The weather was supposed to be good through the time it would take him to complete the project, but on the morning of September 22, storm clouds were gathering. Before he went to work, he spread huge tarps over the top of the house, and he checked the weather report, which forewarned the possibility of scattered showers.

I remember the morning well because I felt almost literally nudged out of bed with the need to go to the temple and stay there as long as possible. The temple is a place of peace, where a separation from the world can offer strength. And I needed both. I returned home to face the realization that being in the temple and unavailable to outside communication had saved me from an incident so stressful that I likely would have gone into hysteria, considering I'd already been so strained.

During my absence, the skies had poured out over an inch of rain in less than an hour. Water ran down our walls in waterfalls, and the carpets became deeply soaked. The insulation and drywall of our upper floor became completely saturated with water, and by evening, the ceiling directly over where I sit to write started to collapse.

The next morning, I packed my car with my pillows, my computer, and a suitcase of essentials, knowing I might not have access to my belongings for a while. A friend drove me to the hospital to have my surgical biopsy, which had been scheduled weeks earlier, while my husband dealt with the insurance company and initial damage control. In addition, thirty or so people from our ward came in and packed up everything on the top floor of the house, which included the rooms where I slept and wrote, and it was all put into a closed-in trailer in our driveway, where I couldn't access it. The entire upper floor was torn out and had to be rebuilt from the rafters down.

The rest of the family found places to sleep in our basement that weren't affected by the flood. But there was no place for me when I returned from the hospital. I lived in a friend's basement for nearly seven weeks, and during that time, I was officially diagnosed with a rare form of breast cancer. The doctor had not been able to get anything close to a clean margin in the surgery, and the more specific lab results left me with only one option: complete, double, radical mastectomy—which meant retracting skin and scraping out every tiny bit of breast tissue they could find.

We all were finally able to move back into our home in November, and I had to try to create a livable atmosphere in my newly constructed space, ignore all of the boxes that had been packed and moved by others in absolute chaos, finish a book that was overdue, complete all of my Christmas shopping, and be prepared to be laid up for weeks.

On December 10, I had my surgery, and it was more difficult than I'd ever imagined. The hard fact was that I hadn't been healthy for years, and I'd already had three surgeries in the last seven months. In March, I had reconstruction surgery, and in April, I had a repair of the reconstruction—which made six surgeries in a year.

At that time, I remember thinking back to my prayers of moving forward on a path to better health, and I was often overcome with feelings of confusion and discouragement. Eventually, I realized God had known my gall bladder was diseased, my neck was about to break, and cancer was lurking in my body.

All of these things *were* an answer to my prayers. But I'm still waiting for the goal of better health to be achieved.

Following my year of surgeries, my health went from bad to worse. My body spiraled down to a place where pain and exhaustion made it increasingly difficult to function—and my creative brain suddenly flat-lined. Losing my ability to write was devastating emotionally since it had always been such a huge part of my identity, but it also meant a harsh financial blow since it was my source of income in a two-income household.

I reached a point where I could no longer attend church, even though doing so had been highly valuable to me my entire life. I could no longer serve in a Church calling or attend the temple. I could no longer go camping or on other outings with my family; things I had done for many years were no longer possible, and I often felt like the people around me were disappointed and confused and not necessarily offering any evidence of trying to understand how all of this might be for me. I had to stop going to movies when the amount of walking gave me added pain for a few days, and additionally, the sensory overload of lights and sound in the theater brought on migraines more intense than the usual, almost-daily migraines. I was battling with my insurance company to get the medication I needed because apparently, "normal" people couldn't possibly have more than nine migraines a month, and I was having them almost daily.

"Have you seen a neurologist about this?" I was asked. "Have you tried this . . . or this . . . or this?"

My answers were that I had tried all of those things and much, much more, and yet it was still a battle to get the medication I needed to be able to barely function.

In the spring of 2013, I first met with the doctor who saved my life. I didn't know I was dying, even though I often felt that way, but lab results quickly showed the disaster going on inside my body. A friend of mine had recommended this doctor months earlier, but it had taken me months to get in to see him. He was technically an endocrinologist, but this man explained things about the effects of Celiac Disease better than the doctors who had diagnosed and treated it years earlier. He was stunned to learn I'd never had a number of things tested in the wake of that diagnosis.

It's a malnutrition disease, which means the body is likely depleted in many ways. Following my diagnosis, I'd had a bone density test and been given iron treatments for anemia. But no other tests had been done. Twelve vials of blood were taken out of me that day, and I went back two weeks later to be shown in black-and-white that several vitamin and mineral levels were completely bottomed out. My hormones were an absolute mess. My thyroid was failing. And I had antibodies in my blood that indicated other food allergies. He also offered a treatment plan for the out-of-control candida that made a great deal more sense than what an infectious disease specialist had recently proposed.

My new heroic doctor started right then to put me on track to getting my health back, and for the first time in years, I felt real hope—even though I knew it would take time. Gradually, the lab work showed improvement, but I was still declining. Over time, my doctor also discovered that my adrenal glands had all but stopped functioning, and I had the MTHFR gene, which caused a great many problems on its own; it was completely unrelated to the Celiac Disease. Though these issues, too, were treated slowly and steadily, I still got worse.

This was the point when I sank into a place where I truly began to lose myself. Who was I if I could be a mother only from my bed, where I spent most of my time? Who was I if I couldn't attend church or serve others? Who was I if I couldn't write? I'd spent years doing a great deal of public speaking, and I'd loved it; I had to let go of that as well. I'd once found respite and enjoyment in going out to lunch with friends, but I could no longer eat where other people wanted to eat, and I'd long ago given up on battling the awkwardness that often came with trying to arrange such things.

Now, going out at all was difficult, but I began to realize my friends were disappearing. A few just couldn't be there as they once had been because circumstances in their lives had changed. But there were others who simply slipped away without explanation, as if my life had become too uncomfortable or depressing for them to handle. One friend I hadn't heard from in many months texted me one day to say how good it had been to see me out walking. I texted back that I could barely walk to the mailbox, so it hadn't been me. And that was it. No follow-up text to ask how I was doing. Nothing. It was as if she could reach out to me believing I was doing better and could be out walking, but since that wasn't the case, only silence followed.

Silence became my worst enemy. In the silence, I felt like a failure, completely inadequate, and hopelessly lost. I felt like a hypocrite given the way I had been speaking to women's groups for years about the need to find value within ourselves no matter what life might throw at us. I had written dozens of novels with themes of rising above life's challenges and becoming stronger, better people by finding our true selves and learning the emotional and spiritual lessons we needed to learn. But I felt like my characters were all disappointed in me, and if my readers knew the reality, they would be too. In my mind, the theme of my life became that I had been given too much that was too hard for too long.

Drawing on my deepest inner strength, I knew that my only true anchor was my faith in the Savior. I was a devout Christian above all else, and I knew I needed to remain firmly rooted in that foundation. There was a great deal I couldn't possibly understand about what was going on in my life, but I knew God knew what He was doing. My connection to Him and my desire to live according to His will had become an ingrained part of me long before I'd ever become ill. My heroes became Job and Joseph Smith—both of whom had suffered incomparable loss and endured unimaginable suffering while feeling isolated or betrayed by friends and loved ones, and perhaps worst of all, they'd felt cut off from the presence of God, questioning from the deepest places of their souls the reasons for such multifaceted struggle while the heavens seemed silent and the reality of this mortal existence could have only felt like hell on earth.

I pondered a great deal the suffering of many people in the world. At times, I would become devoured by shame for feeling sorry for myself when many, many people had it so much worse. At other times, I could recognize that the journey of this life and the experience of personal suffering were very individual, and pain and sorrow might be empathized, but they could not be compared. There was no sliding scale of how difficult an experience might be for one person in contrast to another. My journey was my own, and I had no one but God to turn to for the answers.

Thanks to a doctor who refused to surrender, we never stopped looking for answers. Unlike many doctors before who had told me that since I didn't respond to this or that, nothing could be done, I had a doctor who wasn't just looking for ways to get rid of smoke—meaning, only treating the symptoms—but he was determined to find the fire—the cause of the symptoms—and put it out. Months would pass, and I'd go in for an appointment expecting that he'd be baffled and tell me I had to learn to live with it, but he always gave me hope because he was still searching for answers and had another step I could take that made sense to me because he took the time to explain the treatment, the reasons for it, and exactly what to expect. He treated me like a person; he handed me tissues when I cried.

Still, months passed in between appointments, and even though lab work showed evidence of much improvement in many things, I continued to have more muscle pain, more fatigue, and more weakness; the headaches just kept coming, and many other strange symptoms created new adventures in misery on a regular basis.

In spite of the extreme fatigue to the point of often feeling so tired I could hardly hold my head up or focus enough to read or write, I was almost always too restless to actually sleep. The result was usually that I needed the TV on because I couldn't sleep but also couldn't function mentally or physically enough to accomplish anything else. I enjoyed some amazing movies and television dramas and watched the good ones multiple times. But with the passing of time, I exhausted most of what actually had quality and didn't cross inappropriate lines that would certainly not help me feel any better.

In spite of struggling every day with pain and resulting depression, I had to keep writing because we were now in financial crisis, and my lack of creative drive was irrelevant. Even though I did very little housework—and only in ten-minute increments—I still had to oversee my household and make certain the emotional needs of my family were met.

And still, the weeks and months on the calendar kept passing, and for all of my faith and prayer and efforts to do all I felt right about doing in regard to my health, I only got worse and, subsequently, more prone to depression.

I fought very hard to keep my pain and discouragement from showing when my family members were around. I would pull my best and strongest self forward as much as possible when my married children and grandchildren came to visit. My babies—big and little—were my greatest joy, and I wanted to enjoy every minute of any time together we might have. For those who still lived under my roof, I tried to be honest about how I was feeling, but I still omitted the details most of the time, and I always kept the majority of my suffering to myself.

The worst of my migraines often happened very early in the morning, when no one was awake to witness the depth of suffering. When I needed to cry, I would do it alone. And no one ever saw how many hours I just lay in my bed, staring at the ceiling, or curled up in the fetal position, staring at the wall, almost wishing for a nervous breakdown—or even death. I wasn't even close to suicidal; such thoughts were never in my mind, but that didn't mean I wanted to be alive when years and years of being in pain and feeling mostly useless had worn me down to what felt like a blob of nothingness.

In my heart, I knew members of my family needed me—some more than others—but they were all independent or becoming that way, and my days had only snatches of minutes here and there of talking to them in the midst of their busy lives. I would try to pull myself together for those precious interludes, and I often cried when my bedroom door closed and they went off to resume the normal activities of life while I watched way too much TV because it was the only way I could turn my mind off from all the turmoil running rampant in my thoughts.

So, as life was going on all around me—like a merry-go-round that everyone else was riding while I sat and watched—I prayed and pondered and meditated with the hope of finding answers, and I tried to force myself to do the things that needed to be done that no one else could do. With my inability to go to church or participate in any church-related activities, I watched everything I could find on TV that was spiritually oriented and coincided with my beliefs. But after awhile, I'd seen everything at least twice, and I began to find myself disenchanted with talks and lessons and even the scriptures. I knew the stories of the scriptures well, but I had difficulty focusing enough to reread them without feeling distracted and restless. And for years—in spite of striving to keep an open mind and an open heart—I never heard anything in a talk or a lesson that didn't make me feel like I already knew it, I had already been down that path, or that it was irrelevant to my experience.

At first, I felt guilty for such feelings, until I reminded myself of a principle I knew well: a feeling was just a feeling; it was how I acted on my feelings that determined my character. And the only action I knew to take was to turn to God every single day, to pour my heart out to him, and to reserve some measure of time in silence to try to listen for anything He might offer in return. I was able to accept that I was not having a crisis of faith, for my faith in Christ and His gospel was firm and immovable. I knew Heavenly Father was real and that He was hearing my prayers and would answer them in His own time. I knew the Spirit was real, for I had felt its comfort and guidance all through my life. And I knew angels ministered unto me. I could recount much evidence of these things, and I'd been blessed with miracles and wonders. But these things were most often—as they were with all of humanity—fleeting and difficult to hold on to. Still, the memories of these experiences were clear and undeniable, and my faith was firmly cemented. No, it wasn't a crisis of faith; it was a crisis of hope. And the absence of hope was a dark, dark place.

Somewhere in the midst of this darkness, I gathered my courage and decided to apply a principle I believed to be true: every trial has a lesson. This was not new to me, and I had been looking for the lessons in my trials for most of my adult life. But my trials had never been so severe, and I'd never felt so isolated or depressed; I'd never felt so crippled by pain and illness—in body and spirit. So I took hold of two interrelated principles from the scriptures. The first was the message about the beam and the mote in the New Testament. In essence, the idea was that we shouldn't be focused on the tiny slivers in someone else's eye when we have a beam in our own eye. The metaphor was clear and astounding. How could anyone see *anything* with a beam in their eye?

I found a parallel admonition from the Lord in the Book of Mormon, in Ether 12:27, where we are told that if we ask, the Lord will show us our weaknesses, and if we bring our weaknesses humbly to God, He will turn them into strengths. I took this information as a challenge. I prayed day after day to be shown the beams in my eyes, to be shown my weaknesses so I could turn them into strengths. If I was bound to this bed and could do nothing productive, I was wide open and willing to see what the Lord might teach me. I wanted to learn the lesson in the trial with the hope that the trial would then end.

It took time, but I received those answers. I was guided slowly and steadily through a tutorial of how my weaknesses had been created, some in my upbringing, some in my marriage, some in my profession, etc. I was shown how I had allowed a multitude of things to take place in every aspect of my life that were not healthy or appropriate, and I had been ignoring my instincts and the subtle promptings of the Spirit that had been trying to alert me to the reality that I was not living my authentic life; I was not being true to myself; I was not using my voice as God had intended me to use it—to declare myself appropriately and charitably in all facets of my mortal experience: in business as well as in my personal life, in healing my heart, mind, body, and spirit.

The details of this part of my experience are deeply personally and sacred, but I can say with confidence that we as mortals all have beams in our eyes that block our view of reality, and we usually don't even realize it. I've become keenly aware of the denial and obliviousness of people I come in contact with and how unhappy they are as they avoid the discomfort that could lead them to deeper peace and fulfillment if they would only step into it instead of continually trying to run from it and hide.

I've worked very hard the last few years to apply all I've learned, which I could summarize in three points: First, be charitable to others and to myself—equally. This includes giving others unconditional love—as Jesus would—no matter how much we might disagree with their choices. It also means I must love and respect myself; never put myself above others or others above myself—the latter always having been a challenge. Second, God gave me a voice, and He expects me to use it appropriately and respectfully, with the guidance of the Spirit. Sometimes silence can be empowering, and at other times, it can be destructive. The Spirit will help determine when to speak and when to remain silent, when to just offer love, and when it's important to draw boundaries and not enable others. Third and most important, God's love for us is perfect, absolute, and unconditional, and the Savior's redemptive grace is real.

I have rehearsed these lessons in my mind over and over, asking God to bathe my heart and spirit in them so I can find peace and joy no matter how much pain I'm in or how much money I don't have or how much my loved ones might be struggling with challenges that can break a woman's heart. But still, the pain and depression have continued, other challenges have added heavier burdens, and the peace and joy I have sought so actively and diligently continues to be elusive.

I am learning to live with the fact that two of my children and three grandchildren—so far—also have Celiac Disease. My heart hurts for them, especially these young children who will never be able to eat what everybody else is eating at any school or church or social function. And my daughter Anna, the one with Celiac Disease, has struggled with similar problems to mine; she's not getting better when she should be, and she deals with a great deal of pain and fatigue. Suffering is one thing; watching your child suffer is quite another. Both often feel unbearable. As soon as she was diagnosed with Celiac, I took her to the same doctor I'd been seeing. He helped her put a great many things on track, but like me, she was still getting worse, and we were all struggling for answers.

Through all of this, I found myself asking God quite frequently, "Where is the joy? If we are that we might have joy, then where is the joy? Have I not always strived to live my life according to Thy will? Have I not actively done everything I know how to do that might solve my problems while at the same time looking to Thee for guidance and the miracles of deliverance that can come only from God? Where is the joy?"

I often wondered if there was not some kind of statute of limitations on suffering. I'd seen many people get cancer and suffer greatly from surgery and chemo and radiation, sometimes even going to the brink of death, but then they've come back and healed and have gone on with their lives. And I'm still here, in pain and struggling every day to find any glimmer of joy that will give me hope and help me keep going.

When I realized my daughter Alyssa would be graduating from high school in a few months—and turning eighteen the following week—I fell into a grieving process that took me to a new level of suffering. I'd been sick her entire life, and my year of surgeries had taken place when she was eleven. I'd only gotten sicker since then. I thought of all the things I'd wanted to do with her that had never happened. I thought of the times she had gone to activities and events with a friend and that friend's mother. I'm deeply grateful for the women who have mothered my daughter when I couldn't. But I'm her mother, and I should have been there. I wanted to be there. And now she's all grown up, and she's still going places without me. We're very close, and she's spent a lot of time over the years on my bed with me, telling me about her life and listening to my guidance. She's a wonderful girl, and she's always been kind and patient about my limitations, but my heart hurts over things that can never be relived or replaced—at least not in this life.

Just a few weeks before her graduation, I had a doctor appointment where he told me what he'd suspected for a long time but he'd needed to be certain by process of elimination and many tests. The fact that both Anna and I were seeing the same doctor actually helped him find the answers due to our similar symptoms and similar blood-work results.

We both had Lyme Disease. It was difficult to diagnose and difficult to treat properly, and there was a huge, strange spectrum out there of beliefs regarding the disease, but I felt a deep peace during the hour my doctor explained the proven data of the disease and his method of diagnosis and what would be done to treat it.

The disease explained almost all of my symptoms—and Anna's. He believed I likely got it when I was twelve and had a tick bite and that Anna had gotten it in the womb. To completely get rid of the disease would take about a year, and it usually got much more difficult before it got better. He explained that trying to treat it while both Anna and I had had so many other things wrong would have been too hard on us, but now that we had come this far, the timing seemed divinely orchestrated.

Once again, I went into diagnosis grief, wondering why this couldn't have been discovered a long time ago and why it had caused so much grief for my daughter and me. But the answer was what it had always been: I might not have had any idea what God was doing with my life, but He knew exactly what He was doing, and trusting in Him was absolutely the only way to truly find peace in the face of adversity.

I'm learning ever so slowly how to access that underlying peace the Savior promises; a peace that passeth all understanding. By trusting in the

Lord, we can have that peace no matter how much suffering we might be called upon to endure. In my heart, I have a perfect brightness of hope regarding all things eternal. I know the Savior will deliver on His promises that the Atonement will compensate for all we have lost in this mortal experience. But what about getting through this mortal experience when nearly every hour for so many years has been tainted with pain and depression? And still, I find myself often wondering: where is the joy?

I regularly consider those who live with situations far worse than mine, which helps me keep perspective. I count my blessings every day and strive to remain focused on gratitude, but where is the joy? Joy is not the fleeting happiness that comes and goes with enjoyable events or experiences. Joy, I believe, is something deeper, more abiding, more sanctifying. Joy surely is an irrevocable connection to the faith I have fought to nurture my entire adult life.

And that's the answer: it has been there all along.

I've discovered that joy is like a butterfly that suddenly appears and flutters right in front of us for a few seconds, taking our breath away and making us smile, and then it flies away as quickly as it came. But even when it's no longer in view, the memory of it can make us smile again.

I heard years ago that faith is an action, and hope is a feeling, and one often produces the other. That might be oversimplifying it, but it makes sense to me. And both faith and hope are the main ingredients for joy, and the truth is that when we exercise faith in Christ, hope might be difficult to hold on to, but it will never completely abandon us any more than its Creator. When we have faith in the Savior, we can truly feel a perfect brightness of hope for deliverance in whatever form it might take for each of us as individuals. And along the course of this often terrible and frequently difficult mortal journey, God gives us the gift of joy. It might show up in a funny picture one of my grandkids texted to me that makes me laugh. It might be the bird that decides to play on my windowsill for half a minute. It might be the bouquet of tulips a neighbor leaves on my porch. It might be an unexpected hug from the grandson who doesn't like to hug. And it might be in the appearance of a butterfly, fleeting and elusive but a wonder to behold.

I've also learned another powerful lesson from butterflies. It's important to remember that they were once limited to crawling, and then they were bound in darkness and silence for a period of time before deliverance came and they were able to fly. We as human beings don't want darkness and silence, and we are often very opposed to waiting. But what makes us think we could ever truly be close to God without those elements in our lives?

A part of me wishes I could now say I found another moment of joy when deliverance came and I became healthy and financially secure; however, I am still hoping deliverance is on the horizon. But if I cannot find joy through the course of the trial, I might just miss out on the best moments of my life. I strive to not miss out.

When Alyssa was an infant and my migraines started, I remember wondering how I could possibly enjoy her life when my career was being sabotaged and I was in so much pain, and the Spirit whispered to me that I needed to find joy in her life every day. And so I have. Even when my illnesses have gotten me down, I have found joy in my daughter. I've let go of my regrets over the way life wasn't, even if I might feel some sadness here and there. Instead, I see that this precious girl—and all of her siblings—have given me much joy. And if I'd been as lost in my pain as I sometimes believed I was, I would have missed it.

In chapter forty-two of the book of Job, all things were restored to him and doubled. In April 1839, Joseph Smith escaped from Liberty Jail. And one day, I will step into a new season of life. I've been promised better health in many priesthood blessings, and also a long life. I'm expecting great things of myself because of all I have learned along the way. For what is joy if you cannot share it?

Chapter 6
Finding Joy Amidst the Struggle: A Story of Depression and Anxiety

By Julie Bristow

THE SUNLIGHT SEEPS IN THROUGH the windows as I lay here watching the shadows of the blinds evenly spaced out, reflecting on the wall. At this point in my life, I am pretty good at estimating the time of day by the angle and intensity of the sunlight pouring into the room where I lay. I don't use an alarm most days because even when I do, I just push snooze repeatedly until it stops all on its own. It seems I can exhaust even a piece of electronic equipment to the point that even *it* gives up on me.

An hour or so earlier, my children had come into my room, and we had had several different types of exchanges. One needed help opening a carton of milk they had dragged from the refrigerator in the kitchen all the way down to me in my bed so I could pour it on their breakfast cereal. Another child came in to ask if she could play with a friend, and I told her she needed to do her chores first. My five-year-old twins burst in, fighting about who had had the toy train first. Then I subsequently took it away because they couldn't share it. These exchanges happened all while I still lay in my bed, still in my pajamas.

And the clock is now ticking onward, past eleven o'clock in the morning.

Each time my children walk in and out of my room and close the door behind them, I bury my face in the pillow and try to fall back asleep. And I often succeed, falling back asleep where I feel . . . *safe.*

This scene is normal in my current life. Sometimes, I can carry shame and I struggle with low self-image because of this. I fight hard to battle these feelings of inadequacy. On these frequent, near daily occurrences, it feels as if my bed is holding me captive against my will. It feels as if a 10,000-pound block of steel lies across my body. The heaviness is so relentless. Besides the heaviness, the panic and anxiety start to set in. The panic and anxiety of facing another day is a palpable presence in the air. I try so desperately to breathe in and calm myself down.

My specific diagnosis is called "treatment refractory depression and anxiety," which means conventional methods of treating depression and anxiety don't work for me. We have to think outside the box, as my psychiatrist says. We've tried a number of things. I've been on so many medicines and combinations of medicines I've lost count.

Stress and anxiety are part of life no matter who we are. Stress (and even anxiety) provide motivation to get something done or to overcome an obstacle; however, sometimes it turns into more negative forms, and the very things that can propel us in life can cripple us. My anxiety is categorized under generalized anxiety disorder, which, more or less, means I often feel intense anxiety or panic about nothing in particular. It is simply just there. Anxiety has been more prominent in my life lately than straight depression, even though they go hand in hand as part of a viscous cycle.

Mornings scare me. Mornings are my enemy. Mornings are when I wake up to the reality of my suffering from the reprieve of sleep. There is so much anxiety triggered in the morning that the simple act of the sun coming up triggers a Pavlovian-like response in me of paralyzing fear. Sleep feels like my only escape. What a relief bedtime is, or even a nap, when I can finally drift off to sleep and let the crushing weight of the illness leave by simply being unconscious.

My rational brain knows what is going on. I know this is depression and anxiety. I understand logically that these are symptoms of the mental illness I've dealt with for twenty years. My body, however, feels weak. My emotions and physical capacities feel unprepared to handle the responsibilities of a new day. How much easier it seems to stay in bed, to force myself to fall back asleep. To go back to the unconscious mind that lets go of all the pain, the overwhelming anxiety, the destructive and negative thoughts. And so the battle rages day in and day out. One day, I hope mornings and I will become friends again.

I am often taken aback when I meet people who have never felt what I feel each day. What is life like without this heaviness, this burden, this constant inner turmoil and suffering? I can't really remember—because I have now had this illness longer than I have not.

To the onlooker, I am clearly not crippled. I have full use of my body and limbs. However, the average onlooker cannot see the inside where my mind is often crippled. They cannot see that parts of my brain are not functioning correctly. They cannot see the fear I feel, smell the anxiety coursing through me, taste the depression, or hear the panic that pains my body. Medical professionals, doctors themselves, cannot even do a blood test or a scan to explain my condition. But my condition is still there; it is real; it is tangible, even if only by me. And I know I am not alone. I know thousands, even millions, suffer from mental illness.

I do get out of bed. Finally. I stand up. A knot twists in my stomach, and anxiety streams through my system. I walk through a room of clothes strewn about. A mix of dirty clothes, washed clothes not yet put away, and even folded clothes that haven't made their journey to their respective drawers. I open the bedroom door and proceed down the hallway toward the kitchen, where I hear my children. I trip over toys that lay throughout the hallway and enter the kitchen, whose large, farmhouse sink is overflowing with dirty dishes. Housekeeping is incredibly difficult for me as I often live in survival mode. My ability to focus on a task and complete things has been one of my most frustrating struggles inside this illness. Concentrating does not come easily, whether it is for work or for play. It has robbed me of so many things that I once enjoyed doing, one of which is reading books. My children always come before housework since I often feel incapable of tackling it all, which often leaves us in a messy house, much to my dismay. An untidy house makes the feelings of anxiety and depression worse, but I have to pick my battles and choose where I will put my attention that day.

* * *

There is joy, love, communication, affection, and laughter in this household of mine. My children *know* they are loved, they *feel* my love, and they *act* as though they are enveloped in love. I may not be able to give them an alert, early-morning mother right now or a super tidy household, but there is so much I do have to offer them. I am grateful for the gift of connection I have with those I love the most. The words my children have used to describe me are funny, silly, kind, loveable, helpful, fun, and happy. I *am* that kind of mother to them when I am not severely struggling. Our home is a happy home, despite the opposition that threatens us at times.

I'm ever slowly learning that packing on the shame and guilt does not help—at all. Naming my struggles for what they are, speaking my shame, and dismissing the negative self-talk to the best of my ability are helping set me free. Helping me carry on. Helping me find joy. In my experience, I am taught that joy and pain can coexist. Even though I often feel wrapped in darkness or "anxiety paralysis" (as I call it), somehow a knowledge of hope resides deep inside me. It is that hope that gets me through. One day at a time. I am living, breathing, walking proof of daily struggle and daily joy.

President Russell M. Nelson said, "The joy we feel has little to do with the circumstances of our lives and everything to do with the focus of our lives. . . . If we focus on the joy that will come to us, or to those we love, what can we endure that presently seems overwhelming, painful, scary, unfair, or simply impossible?"[25]

When I reflect on this principle, I realize that sometimes we get to stand in the sun, enjoy its rays, and feel of its warmth and light. Other times in life, we must rely on our memories of that warmth and sunshine. In either situation, there is always room for the light to enter our souls and permeate us with joy. C. S. Lewis said, "If you think of this world as a place intended simply for our happiness, you find it quite intolerable: think of it as a place of training and correction and it's not so bad."[26] So the challenge becomes accepting that throughout our lives, both pain and happiness will coexist, and we must learn to navigate through it.

* * *

I first felt depression and anxiety when I was seventeen years old. Between my junior and senior years of high school, depression and anxiety quietly crept into my life. They crept in without an invite and without warning and gradually spread out their bleak, heavy blanket, choking out the light, the life, and the joy from my once-vibrant self.

I had no reason to be depressed. No trauma, no unpleasant situations or experiences. No environmental factors. Nothing. In fact, my life had been nearly golden. So why, one day, could I not get out of bed? I still don't know the answer to that, but I do know depression and anxiety run heavily in my family. We have the medical history and are genetically predisposed, if you will. My dad still fights this same illness at age seventy-two. He first experienced it when he was the exact same age as me, seventeen years old.

At seventeen, I was the high school junior-class president, a near straight-A student, and surrounded with a good family and amazing friends. I had a

---

25 "Joy and Spiritual Survival," *Ensign*, Nov. 2016.
26 *God and the Dock: Essays on Theology and Ethics*, William B. Eerdmans Publishing Company (1970), 52.

joyful personality and a testimony of my Father in Heaven and His restored gospel. By my senior year, I couldn't get out of bed. I remember missing my morning classes and sometimes even full days of school. My friends teased me that I had "senioritis." I laughed with them while simultaneously feeling hurt and confused inside. I didn't know how to explain to them what was going on because I myself didn't know what was going on. I was just reacting to this strange, new way of *being* as it came creeping in day after day.

My mom eventually dragged me to see a mental health specialist. I remember throwing an epic fit of protest. I screamed, cried, and yelled at her. I didn't want to be different from my peers. I didn't want to have problems. I told her I didn't need medicine and that if I just had enough faith and believed in Jesus Christ enough, He could heal me. *I really thought I could pray my depression and anxiety away.* I remember my mom telling me that Jesus put doctors and medicine here on the earth so the sick could be healed. And so began my journey with medicine, psychiatrists, and counselors—the whole trifecta.

What I didn't know then was that finally surrendering to the fact that I needed help was being brave. In our culture, we often equate being brave with the absence of showing emotion or struggle. That if we can somehow stoically go through our difficulties in life without asking for help or, in my case, without accepting medicine when needed or seeing a counselor, and just keep our poker face on, *then* we are brave. I no longer buy into that way of thinking. Bravery is humility. Humility is one of the most noble of all the Christlike attributes we can attain. Some of the most brave and courageous acts I have seen through others is the ability to push away their pride, show emotion, ask for help, or let their guard down. We don't always have to bottle up our feelings and pretend everything is okay, *especially* if we don't feel okay.

High school graduation came, and I did graduate from high school, though not with the grades I had hoped to graduate with. But I did graduate. That was the beginning of many miracles and tender mercies from the Lord. I continued to be faithful to what I believed to be true, despite feeling awful inside. My struggles, my illness, was not a punishment from God. In fact, it has kept me yoked with Christ.

The Book of Mormon teaches us in Jacob: "Nevertheless, the Lord God showeth us our weakness that we may know that it is by his grace, and his great condescensions unto the children of men, that we have power to do these things."[27] And so, it is by my weakness, my human struggle, that I am reminded of my great dependence on my Savior, Jesus Christ, and my Father in Heaven, the Almighty God.

After high school, I attended and graduated from the University of Utah. A miracle. Part of that miracle was through the American with Disabilities Act. After missing many classes and finding it nearly impossible to focus and study with the raging depression and anxiety, I went to the disabilities office on campus and asked what I needed to do to qualify for help. I was told I needed a note, documentation, and a diagnosis from both my counselor and psychiatrist. I turned in the notes with my diagnosis and recommendations from my doctors and was then put on the disabled list, which, in effect, meant I had extra time to get my homework in and extra time to take tests or turn in projects. I don't know how I would have made it through college without that program.

I graduated college with a bachelor of science degree in human development and family studies. Another tender mercy. It was another lifeline He threw out to help me achieve my dreams to live the kind of life I so desperately wanted despite my limitations and challenges . . . I could not deny God's hand in the achievement of yet another milestone in my life.

After college graduation, entering the full-time workforce was no easy task. I have had a job ever since I was fifteen. But after the depression and anxiety kicked in, there wasn't one job I held where my employer didn't reprimand me for tardiness. Tardiness—because getting out of bed felt next to impossible. It was so humiliating. But for the most part, employers were understanding and compassionate and gave me second chances if our communication remained open. I found it was so important to speak up about my struggles when it was needed. It gave people a chance to give me a chance. It does no good to walk away from something in shame when a conversation usually clears the air. I have learned this lesson, and it has served me well.

* * *

I had fun dating through high school and college. I met Jared in my early twenties, while we were both working as counselors at a Church camp for youth ages fourteen to eighteen. We started dating and fell in love quickly. Two months after we started dating, I told him about my struggles with depression and anxiety. He stayed with me, and he supported me. He saw me

---

27 Jacob 4:7.

at the best of times and at some of my worst of times. While dating, we lived an hour apart from each other. One day, Jared couldn't get ahold of me. As the day passed with no response from repeated phone calls and messages to me, Jared decided he would drive all the way up to my apartment (although inconvenient) to make sure I was okay. My roommate, Allison, let him in. She was unaware of the situation. Jared came up to my bedroom and saw me sleeping. It was nearly 9:00 p.m., and I had been in bed the entire day. I don't even think I had gotten up once to use the restroom. I was comatose with sleep to escape the reality of my struggles. Sleep has always been my "drug" of choice. Jared saw the ugly face of depression that day. He saw it firsthand and still chose me to be his partner. Jared is a good man, good to the very core.

Our dating life and engagement were not easy. Not easy at all. Satan used my already established illness as prey, like a lion preying on a lamb. My mind and heart were confused as I tried to decide if he would be my eternal companion. I would have moments of distinct clarity and would feel like I was making the right decision, but then, when the anxiety and depression were dialed up, my doubt crept back in and became unbearable. The moment we are on the precipice of great things in life is often the moment we get knocked down and feel the most opposition. I've noticed this repeated pattern time and again in my life.

I am a woman who believes in God. But just as God is a reality, I also believe in the adversary, Satan himself. I knew he would try to destroy any righteous, happy, and holy decision I tried to make as I dated Jared. Satan came after me full force. He used all kinds of tactics, such as distraction, apathy, helplessness, depression, anxiety, confusion, contention, shame, frustration, and the list goes on. But I was determined not to let him win. I might have gotten knocked down time and time again, and I might have been on the ground a little longer than I cared to admit, but I rose again, looking toward the true Giver of light, who is Jesus Christ.

As hopeless and bleak as my time spent on the ground felt, I focused on just doing the next right thing. One day, one hour, one minute at a time. I found great comfort in Elder Jeffrey R. Holland's words during this critical time in my life. His words on the reality of Satan, doubt, and retreating from a good thing sang to my ever-searching heart. In a prophetic call and warning from retreating from what we know to be right, he spoke on how the Prophet Joseph Smith was enveloped by darkness right before the most glorious moment of his life, that of seeing God the Father and His Son, Jesus Christ. Elder Holland said,

Most of us do not need any more reminders than we have already had that there is one who personifies "opposition in all things," that "an angel of God" fell "from heaven" and in so doing became "miserable forever." What a chilling destiny. Lehi teaches us that because this is Lucifer's fate, "he sought also the misery of all mankind" (2 Nephi 2:11, 17–18). Surely this must be the original ecclesiastical source for the homely little adage that misery loves company. . . .

This is a lesson in the parlance of the athletic contest that reminds us "it isn't over until it's over." It is the reminder that the fight goes on. Unfortunately, we must not think that Satan is defeated with that first, strong breakthrough that so dramatically brings the light and moves us forward.

Fighting through darkness and despair and pleading for the light is what opened this dispensation. It is what keeps it going, and it is what will keep you going. With Paul, I say to all of you: *Cast not away therefore your confidence, which hath great recompence of reward. For ye have need of patience, that, after ye have done the will of God, ye might receive the promise* [Hebrews 10:35–36].

I acknowledge the reality of opposition and adversity, but I bear witness of the God of Glory, of the redeeming Son of God, of light and hope and a bright future. "Fear ye not." And when the second and the third and the fourth blows come, "fear ye not. . . . The Lord shall fight for you." "Cast not away therefore your confidence."[28]

Heeding these words, not casting away my confidence, and clinging to my moments of light, clarity, and revelation, Jared and I endured the hard times and continued to fight for each other. We dated for a little over a year, and in 2005, we were married and sealed for time and all eternity in the Salt Lake Temple.

Life was and still is hard. Spouses and marriage aren't there to save us or rescue us from our problems. Jared and I learned little by little what our

---

28 "Cast Not Therefore Away Your Confidence," BYU Speeches, March 2, 1999.

new normal looked like and took it one day at a time. We still do. He has his struggles, and I have mine. But we are committed to each other, and more importantly, we are committed to our Savior, our great exemplar, Jesus Christ. The three of us are in this for the long haul.

A few years after we were married, we decided we were ready to try for children. We went on to struggle with the heartbreak of infertility and other health issues. Eventually, we were blessed with three miracle children—our first daughter, Anna, and a few years later, we welcomed boy/girl twins, Noah and Molly, into the world. When the twins were born, we went from one child to three overnight. Because we got what we pleaded and prayed for, I wish I could say it has been bliss ever since. It has been hard . . . really hard. With the birth of each child, feelings of euphoria and excitement came, followed quickly by depression and darkness.

I desperately wanted my children. I had fought hard for them, and I will never forget that fight. But it used to be that just taking care of myself (waking up and showering) was considered a good day for me . . . a hurdle to overcome. Heck, if I brushed my teeth, it was a *great* day. Now I have four people who depend on me. I am a mother and a wife in a family of five. Feelings of inadequacy, shame, and guilt seem to creep into all that I attempt to do. But I am still here and I am doing it. By the grace of God, I am plugging along one day at a time.

Motherhood is a sacred calling and one of my greatest gifts, though it has been such a dichotomy of experiences. It is the great and terrible. The greatest and worst of times. I have never felt so much love and, at other times, so much loneliness. I have felt complete happiness as well as deep sadness. Confusion one day and then clarity the next. Motherhood is beautiful and messy wrapped up in a very untidy package, a wrapping job a three-year-old could have done. I still, to this day, get chills when I hear my little ones say "Mom" out loud. It reminds me that I have had a dream come true. My children keep me on my toes and keep me searching for answers to life's questions. Mothers have God's divinity within them.

I'm finally getting to the point that I'm feeling more joy than struggle with them. Having twins was a rough transition for someone in my shoes, but all the struggle was worth it, even if it took me nearly five years to recognize or feel it. I have to keep reminding myself that God's ways are higher than my ways. I am beyond grateful for all three of my little miracles. I felt God gave me more than I could handle. But He also sent assistance in many various forms. I was sent earthly angels in the form of family, friends, and neighbors who buoyed us up and kept us going those first few years. He loves us. I will forever be grateful that I was given more than I thought I could handle.

* * *

Twenty years after that first encounter with depression and anxiety, I still take medication. I see my psychiatrist every two to three months. We often change things around, adding this, taking away that, or trying something entirely new. I've tried going off medicine as well, and that is not an option for me right now. Every time I try, I crash and cannot function. I am thankful for modern-day medicine to take the edge off, even if it doesn't fully take away my symptoms. No single treatment has ever completely worked for me. I still go to counseling intermittently, and I still need quite a bit of support and help.

This is the way I explain my experience with severe anxiety to those who are not familiar with it: imagine you have just received a phone call from the hospital that your child, your parent, or a sibling has just been in a terrible accident and they are in the operating room. You get to the hospital waiting room, and all you can do is pace back and forth, not knowing whether that person is going to live or die. Essentially, you are in a state of panic for fear of the worst.

Now take those same feelings of fear and imagine feeling that way, but for *no apparent reason*. And you try so hard to figure out why you feel this way but you simply cannot.

Sometimes these episodes lead to paralysis. All I can do is curl up in a ball underneath the covers and ride out the storm.

Despite the tempests, I still feel so much joy in my life, and I realize I have to ride the waves of this struggle, even if I have to do it every day. The Lord, in His infinite wisdom, "seeth fit to chasten his people; yea, He trieth their patience and their faith. Nevertheless—whosoever putteth his trust in him the same shall be lifted up at the last day. Yea, and thus it was with this people."[29]

I have never been suicidal. I don't know why, and I can't explain it. The depths of despair and the discomfort from anxiety have been extreme. I've barely been able to bring food to the table for my kids. I've barely been able to cope and function throughout the day. Periodically, when Jared arrives home from work, I literally see no way out of the pain, so I go to my room and "check out" by trying to fall asleep, exhausted by the mental and physical battle that has been raging in my body all day long.

29 Mosiah 23:21–22.

Feeling physically depleted, lost, numb, and hopeless is the depression side. Then it swings back to anxiety—panic, fear, restlessness, and apprehension. The vicious cycle between the two swaying back and forth on a pendulum I seem powerless to stop. These feelings, this illness, can be pure hell, and I will never discount that for one second. I have felt like I've wanted to die because of the deep, uncomfortable pain and hopelessness. I might be an anomaly with regards to suicide, but I guess I stick to my escape drug of choice: sleep or withdrawing.

When I say things like, "I want to die," it is reminiscent of when we experience extreme misery or pain—like when we've had a bad injury or even a terrible cold, and out of frustration we exclaim, "I just want to die!" What we are really saying is that we want *relief*. And in those moments, seconds, minutes, and hours that matter, I hang on. I hang on for dear life. I hang on for eventual relief. Endurance—even if endurance means I sleep for five hours to rid myself of my horrible pain so I can live the life God has planned for me.

Not too long ago, my five-year-old son said this prayer: "Dear Heavenly Father, please take away my mom's hurts. And help us to have fun tomorrow. In the name of Jesus Christ, amen."

I had been trying to rebound from a pretty severe depressive crash—five days of not being able to get out of bed until evening. This, again, is the ugly face of depression and anxiety. No sugar-coating it. It is what it is. I do feel awful that my children have to witness their mother in these states. I wish I could change it. But I believe in angels. My Savior, my Father in Heaven, and angels administer to my family when I cannot. As well as friends and family who uplift and support. We as a family have also become stronger as we have opened up and communicated about our trials, even talking about Mom's depression and anxiety with our young children.

When I go through these periods of deep darkness and hopelessness, I logically *know* I'll make it through even though it *feels* like I won't. I consider that knowledge of hope one of the greatest blessings of my life, even when I can't *feel* hope. It's a perspective that has taken many, many years with lots of therapy to fully grasp. What knocks us down will truly make us stronger when we are able to get back up . . . if we just let it.

In the meantime, I continue to ride the waves of suffering, like usual, until relief ebbs and flows slowly back in just as the tides of the ocean. Never completely taking it away but giving me pieces of myself back so I can function to the best of my capabilities and soak up the joy life has to offer. Gradually, I start to stand a little taller on my own two feet, picking myself up one piece at a time on nobody's watch but my own. Comparing myself to others has led to only heartache and regression. Just as Theodore Roosevelt said, "Comparison is the thief joy."[30] Those words are so true, and it avails us nothing to compare our weaknesses to others' strengths.

After enduring the darkness, I know heavenly promises come and that there are joys on the other side of that dark tunnel, even when the dark seemed impenetrable. I have felt that dark. I have felt the light. Little by little, I sense that I will see the sunrise again, no matter how many days I have missed it. And I vow to never stop fighting. Through my endurance and patience, I have been granted success in my life.

My days are not all dark. There may be hard parts, particularly in the mornings of each day. But there are good and wonderful parts of most days. We have so much fun as a family. We are a silly family who loves to laugh. We love to have family dance parties, especially in the living room. We read books, have tickle wars, talk in funny accents, watch movies, sing karaoke, build Legos, and cuddle—daily. One of my favorite places in all the earth to be is cuddling with my husband and children. When my children come up in the middle of the night, scared from a bad dream, and need to sleep with Mom and Dad, part of me is secretly a little happy that I get to hold and cuddle them in the stillness of the night. I know they are growing up fast, and I savor their affection and closeness.

My depression and anxiety also seem to lift when I can get outside of the house. We love to hop in the van and go out exploring, finding adventure on the way. Our family makes lists of fun things we want to do each season of the year, and we look forward to them, checking each item off our list. Between an eight-year-old and two five-year-olds, there is so much excitement and zest for life that easily transfers onto me. It may take me until much later in the day to be fully functional, but eventually, the excitement does come. And we have grand adventures. At least, they feel pretty grand to us.

Jared and I also try very hard to make time for a weekly date night to feed and nourish our marriage. The stronger our marriage is, the stronger our family will be. We are twelve years into this marriage, and Jared and I still consider each other our best friend and greatest confidant. We feel grateful and lucky to walk through this life together, surrounded by our children, who are our greatest accomplishments.

30 Dr. Kenneth B. Cooper, Nels Gustafson, and Joseph G. Salah. *Becoming a Great School: Harnessing the Powers of Quality Management and Collaborative Leadership* (December 24, 2013), 9.

You see, when your capacity for deep suffering increases, the flip side is a greater capacity for intense joy. Feeling deeply, even if it hurts sometimes, is one of my greatest blessings. My joy runs deep, as does my pain. I wouldn't change this about my life.

I know I am not alone, and I am not broken, even though I might feel otherwise. As with any physical illness, I continue to seek treatment for my brain. I don't know why it stopped functioning optimally. No one else's actions caused it, and it also wasn't my fault. I'm not sure why the serotonin, norepinephrine, and dopamine in my brain aren't balanced. I don't know why the synapses and neurotransmitters are not doing their job correctly.

What I do know is how I *feel*. I do know how it *feels* to be severely depressed, to have chronic, debilitating, paralyzing anxiety. I do know what it feels like to want to be in bed all day, every day, month after month, year after year. But I also know that this is my fight to fight. I've accepted that, and I'm trying my best to show up for life each day that I can.

I continue to be a student of bearing with patience mine afflictions.[31] I have not always done it with grace, but I have seen time and again the success the Lord has given me as I continue to endure to the end. I might often be down, but I'm still fighting. Every single day. By showing up for life each day and battling my illness, the glimpses and feelings of joy are becoming longer and more lasting. As much as I talk about hope and joy, I do not always *feel* hope and joy. I don't have the relationship with the Holy Ghost that I wish I did, because often, the very faculties to reach my Father in Heaven are the ones that are crippled. That is where obedience comes in—remaining true to my covenants and having faith in Heavenly Father's promises so my *knowledge* of hope and joy can carry me through on my darkest of days, when feeling anything like joy just isn't possible. That knowledge carries me through.

My testimony of Jesus Christ and this gift of endurance is given only in and through Him. So hope remains. Not necessarily hope that this trial will be taken away from me permanently but hope that I can continue to endure, endure it well, and find joy amidst the pain.

---

31 See Alma 38.

PART IV: FAMILY

Chapter 7
100% Treatable: Overcoming Postpartum Depression and Anxiety
By Lindsay Aerts

I COULD FEEL THE WARM glow of the fire on my face as I sat one snowy December day at my family's cabin in Maine. I wasn't doing anything of particular importance when all of the sudden, a thought flashed through in my mind. It was a terrible, horrible, rather vivid thought about harm coming to my then two-month-old baby girl. It felt very real, almost like I pictured myself doing it. It bombarded me out of nowhere, and I instantly felt horrible that a thought like that was even capable of crossing my mind. It certainly felt like a weird thought to have and was more vivid than the rest, but I shook it off, ignored it, and moved on with my family vacation before I starting back to working full-time as a radio host after my maternity leave.

* * *

Lucy was born on October 17, 2014, and my maternity leave seemed to be going well. Over the next twelve weeks, though, I struggled with the newborn-baby-lack-of-sleep exhaustion, coupled with the emotional and physical toll of breastfeeding—believing the fallacy that every time I had to give her formula, I failed at giving her the best chance at a healthy life. The shame associated with not feeding her what was "best," the guilt over the cost of formula when breastmilk was a free source of food, the excruciatingly painful mastitis, the surgery at four weeks' postpartum to drain the clogged duct in my breast, the around-the-clock pumping to keep up my supply of milk, the cluster feeds, the weight of now being responsible for another human life and responsible (so I thought) for how that life would turn out, the need to check on her every minute to see if she was breathing, the endless "what-ifs" spinning in my head—all this made for a rough introduction to being a mom.

I would later learn that all these things, combined with the stress of going back to work an eight-hour day when I was already so overwhelmed, plus the stress of feeling so utterly alone when my husband's job kept him working past midnight every night, was a recipe for disaster. A postpartum anxiety and OCD disaster.

This could not be the joy of having a baby that everyone talked about. I felt bitter about all the lovely, wonderful "I'm so in love" new-baby photos I saw everywhere. I loved my baby desperately, but I was miserable. Looking back, I can see where some of my anxieties first manifested, but the OCD really took hold about three months postpartum when I started having more of the scary, intrusive, unwanted thoughts about harm coming to my baby, often at my own hand. Not knowing what they were, I started to spiral out of control.

One day after doing a live broadcast from a business in Utah County, I was driving home, feeling piercing anxiety about all these thoughts swirling through my head. "What kind of mother has thoughts like this? I must be a monster. Am I capable of hurting my baby? If I think these things, doesn't that mean I'm capable of doing them?" At the time, I falsely thought I would.

When I got home, I broke down to my husband. I asked him to take me to the hospital. I told him I needed morphine. I needed something to make all these awful thoughts go away. I felt trapped inside my own head. I stopped functioning. I took two days off of work. I stayed with a cousin so I didn't have to be alone with my baby. I was terrified of my own brain. That was when I knew I needed professional help.

I believe that healing from a postpartum mood or anxiety disorder is more than just choosing to think positively or choosing to be grateful or counting your blessings. This is an illness. Healing the mind first and foremost is so vitally important in being able to choose joy. We wouldn't just try to think positively to heal a broken leg. We would go to the doctor, get a cast, and make sure the bone healed before we tried to run again. The same is true for healing mental illness and healing the mind.

Postpartum mood and anxiety disorders are agitated illnesses, meaning that depression and/or anxiety are triggered by an event (like the birth of a child), combined with any biological (family history of mental illness), environmental (stress), sociological (cultural beliefs), and physiological (hormonal) factors. There's no one cause; thus, there's no one cure. These disorders can happen anytime during pregnancy and/or the first year postpartum.

Trust me—logically knowing you want to feel better, that you want to just feel joy, and knowing how grateful you are to God for your healthy, beautiful child only make the fact that you can't feel better even worse.

Not only was I scared that I was going crazy, but I was also worried that the anxiety was coming back. I ruminated, thinking these thoughts on a seemingly endless loop. These intrusive, obsessive thoughts were the main symptom of my postpartum OCD. Some women also have compulsions, like excessively washing hands, bottles, or cleaning. Subsequent anxiety and depression typically follow.

Many moms don't seek help because we might think no one can be having scarier thoughts than us, so we don't want to admit to them. We are so scared of someone thinking we really might be crazy or, worse, question if we're fit to be a mother that we keep quiet.

The book *Dropping the Baby and Other Scary Thoughts* taught me it's not the content of your thoughts that are the problem but the amount of distress they cause that needs to be treated. This was the beginning of my journey to joy.

At one point, I realized that the fact that these scary thoughts caused such anxiety was actually a good thing. It meant that I knew the difference between right and wrong and that was why the thoughts felt so awful. They were inconsistent with who I knew myself to be. Logically, I knew I never wanted to act on any of these scary thoughts, but because of how real they felt, they made me think I was capable of the actions. Insert *anxiety, panic, dread,* and *fear* here.

In trying to avoid the anxiety that the thoughts were causing, I avoided being anywhere alone with my baby. The harder I tried not to think about the scary thoughts, the more they would come back. You know, the classic "If I tell you not to think about a pink elephant right now, what are you thinking about?" Suppression and avoidance of thoughts or emotions didn't make them go away. There were physical symptoms too. I was nauseated and not eating, and I felt physically ill from the anxiety and the fear of when a scary thought would hit again. My mind was on a constant loop of thoughts, like, "What if I just snap and do the things I am thinking?"

I didn't. I was never going to. Those scary thoughts lasted about a month and a half. I had to treat the anxiety associated with them before I could address underlying issues though.

As I stated before, underneath it all, I was completely overwhelmed by the thought of caring for another human being. This wasn't the type of overwhelmed where I could just do less in my day because I was doing too much, although that was, indeed, helpful. This was a deep-seeded fear of not knowing how to take care of a child when I'd been under the impression that this knowledge would come instinctively to me as a woman. A mother's intuition just kicked in, right? I felt like I didn't have the chip, the gene, to be a mom. No one ever told me there was even a possibility of feeling anything but happy after a baby was born (or maybe they did, and I just didn't hear them). So I continued to carry around all that shame, thinking I was a broken, defective mother.

People who talk to me about this experience often want to know how long healing from a postpartum mood and anxiety disorder takes, and I wish so badly I could tell them specifically. I always used to say I could gear up for the fight if I just knew how long it would last. Healing comes in cycles, slowly and over time. Good days start to outweigh the bad. The thoughts fade.

How did I heal? My biggest helps were medication, therapy, taking kid-free breaks, and sunshine. Experts also talk about exercise, proper nutrition, reading, praying, walking, writing—basically, anything and everything that brings relief is what a mom should do . . . and keep doing, even after she starts to feel better! I completely understand why they advocate for these things, and I chose to focus on a few that I found brought me the greatest and most immediate relief. I also mourned the losses of my old life as I began to process my new life as a mom—the things I gave up, like sleep, naps, my body, the amount of stress I could now handle, and my independence. I allowed myself to feel sad that I was not the person I was before I had a baby, and I did not resist or feel guilty for feeling this new way. This didn't mean I didn't love my baby or want her here. It meant I learned these pre-baby luxuries were not mine now but were not necessarily gone forever, and I could find a new normal.

My support system became key in helping me heal. I would text my mom or husband a code word to let them know I'd had a scary thought, and they would call me and ask me to say the thought out loud. That would take away its power. They knew the person I was before having postpartum issues, and they could remind me of that.

Postpartum mood and anxiety disorders are 100 percent treatable, though I don't want to simplify the healing process. Grueling hours of therapy to really dig down and figure out the thoughts I was believing that were causing me such pain took a lot of emotional work. Hard work.

Work is required to find joy too. Emotional, sometimes painful, shell-cracking work. You know the expression "Happiness is a choice"? I believe happiness is not only a choice but a skill that we practice over and over. In my mind, that's true for finding joy too. This skill, though, can only really be effectively implemented if there are no other factors at play, such as mental illness. Sometimes you can't simply choose or practice joy if your brain is somehow preventing that. As humans, our brains are hardwired for survival, meaning they are always looking out for danger; they're trying to protect us from both physical and emotional danger. That suggests we're almost always looking out for negative situations to protect ourselves from them so we can avoid them at all costs. Although our brains are wired to find what's wrong, they can also be conditioned to look for what is right. Many of us will thus have to consciously override the protective nature of our brains in order to feel joy. That is tough work.

I think for a long time, I expected to just feel joy. I didn't have many trials, and I didn't have a ton of challenging hardships. I had so much to be grateful for, so I should have felt joy.

But it doesn't always work like that. You can't just tell yourself to feel joy and expect all the bad emotion to part and the sun to shine again. If you have a chemical imbalance in your brain, you certainly can't just will yourself to feel joy. If you had asked me to feel joy in the middle of crippling postpartum anxiety and OCD after my first baby girl was born, I would have told you to go jump in a lake.

I've since come to learn that the subconscious mind is driving a large percentage of the time, so if I was not choosing thoughts that helped me feel joy, it was not necessarily going to become my default setting.

I now subscribe to a new way of thinking that helps tremendously in helping me curb anxieties. I have come to understand it's not just my circumstances that cause my feelings but rather a combination of my circumstances, other people's actions, and even my past. My feelings drive my actions, and my actions are creating the results in my life. This sounds nuanced, but this little formula has been life-changing for me in finding joy. I know I can't always choose what thoughts pop into my head, but I can choose whether or not I believe the ones that do. So despite what's going on in my life, I now have more confidence that I can handle any emotion because I can examine the thinking behind it. For me, joy is now knowing I can handle negative emotion because I know what to do with it, being grateful to God for all I have, and living consciously—meaning, paying attention to my thinking because those thoughts are what cause my feelings.

Emotion is not a danger. It won't kill me, even if it feels like it will. Am I scared to have another baby? You bet. Do I want another postpartum illness? No, thank you. And I'm at a high risk of having one again because I've had one before. My biggest fear, though, is the anxiety that comes with my postpartum. I'm scared of how bad it could feel. But the truth is, I can do feelings. That doesn't mean I'm not scared; it means I now know how to handle being scared.

In addition to knowing how to handle emotion, I have to make sure I control the self-judgment that can wreak havoc on my mind. You know that little voice in our heads that says, "You're not good enough; you're not smart enough; you're not pretty enough"? She can steal my confidence. She still does at times if I don't pay attention to her. She can convince me I'm not a good enough mom, that I shouldn't have written in this book, that I'm not being spiritual enough—even that I don't believe in God enough. I now pay attention to her. This allows me to override her negativity. I can tell her, "Thank you for informing me of what you think, but I'm going to choose to believe otherwise." I know I get to choose to believe anything I want, and I choose joy.

I share my postpartum OCD story simply because not many women do. I've heard it said, "Be kind, for everyone is fighting a battle you know nothing about." If you ever hear me on the radio and everything seems fine, it very well might be because joy is something I'm constantly choosing. I think joy is a feeling you can always access, but it takes work to choose it. I believe it's what God wants for us. The scriptures tell us that "men are that they might have joy."[24]

I believe God is in the details of our lives. My postpartum journey has led me to new tools I can now access if and when other adversity happens, it has taught me how to have empathy for other mothers, and it continues to teach me how to accept all emotion without self-judgment or shame. This brings me godly confidence. I have learned I can handle any situation life throws at me because negative emotions are not bad; they're part of the journey. God wants me to feel joy, He is rooting for me, and I know He is rooting for you too.

---

24 2 Nephi 2:25.

Chapter 8
Mother of Joy: The Story of Nathan Glad
By Rachel Glad

BEING NATHAN'S MOM HAS NOT been easy; in fact, it has been downright hard. It is heart breaking, challenging, and lonely. But being his mom has proven to be the most amazing, uplifting, and joyous thing I have ever done.

Let me start at the beginning, before Nathan was even born. My husband, Ryan, and I were in an ultrasound room. Our daughter, Courtney (then almost two years old), was being cared for by a grandparent. We could see in the ultrasound that we were having a baby boy, and we were thrilled. My previous pregnancy was a miscarriage, so seeing a baby boy on the screen was such a blessing. As the examination continued, we noticed the technician measuring and remeasuring and remeasuring again. This seemed unusual. Did she not know what she was doing? She stepped out for a while, then came back in and measured yet again. Then she cleaned off my stomach and said that my doctor would be contacting us with the results.

My OB at the time was Dr. Smith. He contacted me and informed us that the baby's femur bones were measuring small, and this was concerning. He scheduled us for another ultrasound in a month. At twenty-four weeks, I went in for a second ultrasound, and the femurs were still measuring short. No one would tell us what this meant. Starting to fear for our son, Ryan and I began praying. Patience always seemed to be our answer. Being an impatient person, this really frustrated me. But having no choice, I waited to learn more. I am grateful to my beautiful Courtney for being my distraction during this time of not knowing.

I was referred to a perinatologist, Dr. Rose, at LDS Hospital in Salt Lake City. She specialized in diagnosing in-utero babies. After the ultrasound with her, she explained to us what the short and now bowed femur bones meant to her. It was evidence that our baby had some form of skeletal dysplasia, or a bone disorder. Most likely, it would be achondroplasia or osteogenesis imperfecta (OI). The bowing of the bones signified fractures. As our visits progressed, Dr. Rose was more confident in the OI, or brittle bone disease, diagnosis, as the bones continued to bow and show possible fracturing.

In that first visit with Dr. Rose, our world crumbled. The original vision of a healthy, bouncing baby boy disappeared. It was replaced with more fear and anxiety. Dr. Rose then brought up the option for termination of the pregnancy. The question sounded like a gunshot. Our baby's condition was serious enough to offer such an extreme measure. We told her immediately that this was not an option for us, and she never brought the subject up again.

My pregnancy was wrought with nonstress tests, ultrasounds, and meeting with professionals that would help in the delivery of my sweet boy. Things were going as planned until Halloween of 2006. We arrived at our stress test and were met by the neonatologist who would be there to care for our son. This was according to plan. We were putting together a birthing plan so we could know exactly how things would go. We were to deliver the baby at LDS Hospital right next to the Newborn Intensive Care Unit (NICU). And this was the woman who would take and care for him there, if needed.

After she introduced herself, she asked very bluntly, "Where would you like your baby to die?"

What? Did I hear her right? I never thought that was a possibility. I was planning on bringing my baby home—maybe not the healthy baby we had hoped for but a baby, nonetheless. My monitors for the stress test started going crazy.

In tears, Ryan explained that we expected to deliver and keep a living baby. Counselors rushed the doctor out of our curtained area and helped calm us down. They made sure my contractions were not productive and set us up with grief counseling before sending us on our way. I never knew a heart could break so much.

Dr. Rose had studied our last ultrasound and had determined that the baby's spine was now curving in such a way that when his lungs expanded, there would not be enough room for him to breathe. If he was able to take his first breath, there would not be many more after that. She had relayed that information to the staff and was waiting to see us in person to explain her findings. Unfortunately, she was out of town and had not been able to talk to us before the neonatologist had visited with us.

Completely devastated, we had to pick ourselves up and take care of Courtney. It was Halloween, and she was so excited to go trick or treating. We did not want to burden her with our grief.

I was under doctor's orders to take it easy, so I helped dress her in her little purple butterfly costume, and Ryan took her out while I stayed home to rest and pass out candy. I called my mom to tell her the news. I didn't know how to get the words out, but somehow, I managed to tell her that the doctors didn't think our baby would make it. Her response got me thinking.

She said, "I am going to pray that he lives. Because if all I have to do is ask to be his Nana, I'd better ask!"

It was a powerful thought. Had I asked my Heavenly Father to let me be my son's mom? I started asking, begging, and pleading to be his mother. If my Father in Heaven could send Nathan to this earth and he could have a good quality of life, I really wanted to be his mother. I did not want him to come and suffer because of my selfishness, but if he could be happy here with me, I truly wanted that.

Later that night, Ryan brought a candy-filled Courtney home. Despite our solemn mood, she had still enjoyed her evening. On their walk, they had stopped by our bishop's home, Bishop Kitchens. He invited Ryan in and talked with him for a minute while Courtney played with his dear wife. He offered to come to our house later that evening and help give me a priesthood blessing. When the bishop arrived at our house, he expressed his love and concern for our little family. He then gave me one of the most powerful blessings I have ever had. He spoke of the plan of salvation and taught me again that if I was not able to raise my children now, I would have that opportunity in the future. He also referenced the Psalm 23.

After closing the blessing, Bishop Kitchens asked me how I felt. I told him I felt I was being educated and prepared for all possibilities, but now was not the time for me to know if my son would live or die. He looked baffled at my response and stated, "It's your blessing."

That night, I could not sleep. I studied the twenty-third Psalm. I pored over it and looked up cross-references and read and reread them. I followed a chain that seemed to be answering my questions of what I needed to do if I was not to know the outcome. The scriptures that brought me peace said, "And he also said unto him: If thou wilt turn unto me, and hearken unto my voice, and believe, and repent of all thy transgressions, and be baptized, even in water, in the name of mine Only Begotten Son, who is full of grace and truth, which is Jesus Christ, the only name which shall be given under heaven, whereby salvation shall come unto the children of men, ye shall receive the gift of the Holy Ghost, asking all things in his name, and whatsoever ye shall ask, it shall be given you."[32]

As I read this, I felt *again* the impression to ask. I had been baptized, I had received the Holy Ghost, and I felt I had not made any major transgressions in my life that were unresolved. I had always been a "good girl." I needed to ask; I needed to keep asking, and I never stopped having that prayer with me. If I could be his mother and he would be happy, I wanted to be his mother!

The next weeks were extremely hard. Grief counseling started, and we began making funeral home arrangements. We also decided we needed to stop calling him baby boy in our prayers and needed a name for ourselves and others to pray for. The name we decided on was *Nathan Ryan Glad*.

My cesarean section was scheduled for November 17. During this time, most are excited to have a new baby join their family. People often asked if I was excited to have my baby. I struggled to answer those questions. I knew under normal circumstances, I would be excited, but I didn't want to explain why I was anxious. If possible, I would have kept my Nathan inside me forever. Especially if it meant he would live. I could feel his tiny body moving and never wanted that to stop.

The social stress was almost unbearable, and the preparations for a funeral were nearly impossible.

At 3:00 a.m. on Sunday, November 12, 2006, my water broke. It was a slow, uncomfortable leak. Ryan rushed around, grabbing everything we needed. Earlier that night, I'd had the impression to pack the hospital bag for the delivery. Ryan had looked at me strangely as I'd gathered things, because Nathan wasn't coming for another week, but I'd just kept going with a feeling that I really needed to do this. Looking back, I was grateful I had followed that inspiration.

Ryan grabbed my bag and met his parents outside, who were going to take care of Courtney for us. Once a sleepy Courtney was on her way, we headed to the hospital.

Contractions were starting, but they never did cause me much pain. Dr. Rose met us in the hospital room to finalize everything. She had autopsy forms with her for me to sign. We had agreed to allow for an autopsy on his body but not his head. This would then allow for us to bury our Nathan. We

---

32 Moses 6:52.

also told them we wanted Nathan to go to the NICU only if they really felt they could save his life. Otherwise, we wanted to hold our baby and say good-bye. I really wanted to hold him alive, even if it was for only a few seconds.

As they prepped me for surgery, my soul felt like it existed somewhere outside my body. I was so numb to what was happening to me. I started shaking uncontrollably. It was as if the emotions of the day had put me into shock. Nurses wrapped me in warm towels and tried some meds to help steady me. Eventually, I stopped shaking, and the surgery began.

Nathan was born just after 8:00 a.m. on Sunday, November 12. They rushed him to the tiny area set up to assess him. They placed a little nasal cannula by him, and miraculously, that was all it took, and he started crying. It was the most beautiful sound I had ever heard. It was not a loud cry, but it was strong. They wiped Nathan off a little and wrapped him up and handed him to Ryan. Ryan then brought me our sweet little boy.

Never have I felt such pure joy! My prayers were answered as I snuggled our Nathan. He was tiny, only five pounds. He had his little leg up by his ear, but no one dared force it down. He was pink and had black hair. He was beautiful, and I could hold him and be his mom. No one knew how long we would have with him, so we treasured each minute.

One minute led to another and then another. This boy was not going anywhere!

It took a good two days before the doctors agreed. I felt like I was float-ing. I would stare at his perfect little cheeks and stroke his perfect little head.

About an hour after Nathan's birth, we gave him a name and a blessing in the hospital. There were very few in the circle: Ryan, who gave the blessing; my dad; Ryan's dad; and my brother. The blessing was short and beautiful. It just said that Nathan would be here on the earth long enough to complete his mission. Little did we realize that that mission would be over the course of the next ten years.

In the years following that day, I have had the privilege of being Nathan's mom. I have seen him genuinely sad maybe twice and only for a few hours. He does get frustrated and struggles with pain daily, but he is hardly ever depressed. This is because Nathan chooses each day to be happy. He has a mantra he lives by that he developed shortly after he could talk. It is "Today is the best day ever!" When asked what tomorrow will be, he says, "It will be the best day ever because every day is the best day ever." He has infused this motto into our family, and we try to live with every day being the best.

The first thing I learned raising Nathan was how much I took for granted! When he smiled at me for the first time, I bawled! I never thought I would see that beautiful smile! And Nathan has been smiling ever since.

He has struggled to reach every milestone. But through his struggles, he keeps smiling and trying.

Nathan figured out how to crawl on his back and wiggle like a snake. When he made it out of my bedroom and started down the hall, we celebrated! His head was too heavy to lift while on his belly, but that wasn't going to stop this boy from getting from place to place.

His struggles seem to provide the perfect dark contrast to the bright light of his joy. His body doesn't grow like a typical child's. His head grows but his body did not. His body worked harder to heal micro fractures and broken bones. He is considered a little person. His head size would barely make the pediatrician's growing charts while his weight and height would never even be close to being on the chart. He was growing but very slowly.

Now, as a ten-year-old, Nathan is only thirty-two inches tall, twenty-seven pounds, and wears 3T clothing and an adult-size ballcap. Being a little person makes things challenging, but it never stops him. We just adapt.

Nathan was officially diagnosed with osteogenesis imperfecta about six months after he was born, by skin biopsy. He is strong but fragile. He breaks a bone, typically a long bone, every month, on average. The breaks are painful and take weeks to heal. I have learned how to splint and care for his fractures at home. We rarely get x-rays now because we know it is broken, and more than half won't even show up on x-ray because they are hairline fractures.

When he was a baby, Nathan would break a bone just rolling over in his sleep, coughing, or having a muscle spasm. Many times, we would not know what caused the fracture, but because of the extreme pain, we knew it was broken. Nathan can now communicate when something hurts and what might have happened.

There is no cure for OI, but he can get a bisphosphonate IV infusion regularly to help increase his bone density and help alleviate some of the chronic pain he faces daily.

His treatments also include rodding surgeries to help straighten and strengthen his long bones. They break the bone to straighten it and place a rod down the center to help give strength and act as an internal splint. We first tried this treatment when Nathan was two years old. At the time, we were in what is called a fracture cycle with his femur. He would break it, and as soon as the splint was off again, he would break it again. This had been going on for months, and we didn't know how to stop the cycle. Femurs are largest bones in the body, and when they break, it is one of the most painful fractures. Along with a femur fracture, many times it is followed by muscle spasms. These spasms hurt worse than the initial fracture and can occur as often as every five minutes. This is why we decided to try the rodding surgery.

It was the first time I had to send my little man back into surgery. It felt like they were ripping my heart out and taking it away. Ryan and I just held each other and prayed. Nathan's orthopedic surgeon came to talk with us after the surgery. It had not gone well. Nathan was fine, but the rod could not be placed. Each time they would go to place it, the bone would crumble and melt away. They tried a couple of times but soon decided they were causing more harm and closed him up. The doctor sat and cried with us. Our boy was placed in a hip spica and would have to rebuild his femur.

When we could see Nathan again, he was in so much pain. It took three days to get it under control. His spasms were excruciating, and sleep was impossible. All we could do was hold him, talk to him, and pray.

That surgery was December 22, 2008, and he was not able to go home until December 26. Our son, Jason, spent his very first Christmas in the hospital. I really wanted our family home for Christmas, but with prayer and love, I realized that holidays, while special, could be put on hold. We celebrated a few days later.

The rod could not be placed, but the fracture cycle did stop. Our doctor said that in two decades of practice, he had never seen such fragile bones. This was one of our lowest moments. Others would come. We have realized we cannot experience and appreciate the joy without the lows.

Eventually, Nathan's smile returned, and after some years of growth passed, his legs were rodded. Nathan learned some very beneficial breathing techniques that have helped him get through the extreme bouts of pain.

Nathan has never been able to support his weight or stand on his own. He is a wheelchair user and *loves* the speed and ease of his power chair. He was fitted for his first chair at Shriners Hospital for Children—Salt Lake City when he was eighteen months old and received his first power chair at three years old, again from Shriners. At first, he was nervous and scared of the chair, but that was shortly overcome, and now he speeds around his school with the other kids—happy as can be.

The chair has also allowed him to enjoy his favorite sport, baseball. He plays on a sponsored Miracle League Team, the Angels. You can see the pure joy on his face as he hits the ball and pushes the little joystick forward and those little legs start kicking and running as fast as they can all the way to first base. He absolutely loves baseball. He takes his game very seriously and doesn't want to let anyone on his team down.

One day, right before a game, Nathan was in a small accident where his wheelchair tray fell down on him. This resulted in two broken arms and a broken leg. We were at someone else's house at the time and were headed to the game right after our visit. Of course, when this happened, we told him we would take him home to rest. He would have none of that.

"No," he said. "I need to go to my game!"

So we took him to the game and explained to his coach what had happened. They lovingly told him it was okay and that he was fine to go home to heal. Nathan, in excruciating pain, finally agreed to let us take him home but only after he knew it was okay with his coach.

Nathan's ability to overcome is truly an inspiration. He has had a will to succeed and accomplish his assignments from a very young age. One day while walking to his preschool class, we hit a curb wrong with his wheelchair, and his body shifted forward. The belt kept him in his chair, but he did end up breaking his femur. Instantly, he started screaming, and I helped him back into a seated position. I was about to turn around to go home so I could splint it and give him pain meds, but again, Nathan would not let me. He told me he needed to turn in his assignment to his teacher. I tried to explain that if he was crying and in so much pain, it was better to go home and that his teacher would understand if he turned it in later. But Nathan would not give in. He sucked up his tears, put on a smile, and told me to push him the rest of the way to school. We turned in his papers, picked up Courtney, and walked home. Not one tear fell until we got home. His mental strength is incomparable.

When he puts his mind to something, he makes it happen.

Most of his life is spent in some sort of splint or wrapping. His fractures aren't casted because the weight of the cast will cause another fracture wherever the cast starts or ends. He can also never have his bones set because they are too fragile, and again, it would cause more breaks.

When family or friends see him in a splint, they'll sometimes say, "Oh bummer, you have another broken arm!"

His response is sweet. "It's okay; I still have this one!" And he'll raise his free arm and wave. No matter how awful the situation, he finds the joy in it.

As a young child, when he would pray in our family prayers, he would often include thanks to his Heavenly Father for his body. This was so powerful to me. I know, even now, I am very critical about my appearance and have struggled with self-esteem and body image. This little boy just sees the world and everything in it as a blessing and an opportunity, even his fragile little body. These have been powerful learning moments for me.

With all our family's struggles, we have found a priceless treasure in local charities. When Nathan was four years old, we were introduced to a group called Angel's Hands Foundation. This group was formed to be a support to families who deal with rare conditions. The founder, Mark, had a child with a rare condition and understands how lonely and expensive it can be raising a child who doesn't fit into any group. The people in this group understand. They know the difficulty of getting a van full of equipment ready and loaded just to go grocery shopping. They empathize with the feeling you get when other kids look at your child and call them a freak. They know how it is to show up to a kindergarten class, where the kids are in PE and playing a game that can injure your fragile boy, and you must take him home crying because all he wants to do is play. They understand the exclusion your son feels because he cannot join in a game or play a simple game of tag. They help us navigate life and help Nathan understand. The foundation has created a safe place for our kids to enjoy incredible opportunities. They have held hockey nights, Christmas parties, swimming parties, and bike rides. And each of these activities is adaptable to the child's needs and includes the entire family.

One of the hardest parts of having a child who is so different is seeing our other children miss out on opportunities because of hospital stays and fractured bones. They also see people reach out to Nathan. The people adore him and give him presents, but many times, my Courtney and Jason are just left to watch. I have been truly blessed with amazing children, though, who understand and never complain when Nathan gets that extra attention. All the same, allowing them to enjoy an activity too is such a blessing. Mark has always said, "It is the whole family that lives with the condition, not just the child who has the condition." The whole family has to make sacrifices. But with those sacrifices, we have found joy!

One time of joy came on a family vacation. Our family saved for three years to go to Disneyland. We had a blast. In 2012, we stayed in one of the Disneyland hotels and spent five days enjoying this magical time. While we were there, another local Utah charity contacted us, inviting us to a baseball game. Nathan was to be the first child that the Sons of Baseball would take to a game. It was so incredible. Our family arrived at Angel Stadium, and we were greeted with bags of swag and jerseys for everyone. I remember taking

Nathan into the bathroom to change into his new Angel's jersey, and he came out exclaiming, "Now I am a professional baseball player!" We were able to go on the field and watch batting practice, visit with the coaches, and have balls signed. Nathan went into the dugout and took some bubble gum from their stash. We visited the press box and watched a great game. The Angels scored the homeruns Nathan had asked for and won the game. Afterward, we watched the fireworks light up the sky right over the Big A on the stadium. This trip was truly magical and a happy memory we revisit often.

Just a short year later, Nathan was asked if he wanted to go on a make-a-wish trip. He, of course, told them about our magical Disneyland trip and informed them he now needed to see Mickey's other home in Florida. This family vacation would never have happened if anonymous people hadn't opened their hearts and allowed these charity groups to do what they do so well. Other groups that have helped us are The Mascot Miracles Foundation, Children and the Earth, and Shriners Hospital for Children—Salt Lake City.

These groups have become our family. We laugh, cry, and support each other. We have met the kindest, most loving people who would be there for our family in a heartbeat. The joy they bring to us would not have been realized had we not had Nathan in our family. Joy is found in not only receiving but also trying to give back to these groups. We show up early to events, when possible, and help set up. We collect donations for auctions, plan and organize events, volunteer any way we can, and help these groups do what they do. This service has brought our family so many blessings. We have formed lasting relationships, and we know we will be taken care of. When Nathan needs them, a prayer network goes to work, and everyone everywhere says prayers for him. His service and desire to share his joy invite love and joy for others.

When Nathan was six years old, we were introduced to Dallas Graham, founder of the Red Fred Project. This was a new idea Dallas was trying, and he was directed to us to help him start. He wanted to help children with life-threatening conditions write and publish books. Nathan became Dallas's first creative. They wrote this beautiful book called *Climbing with Tigers*. It is all about a little black bird named Blue who is too afraid to fly because he has Brittle Bones. Dallas's Jolly Troop comes to help Blue, and together, they go on a magical adventure.

Writing this book was an exciting time for our family. Right after the book was published, Nathan was invited to a book signing, where he signed book after book for hours. He shares this book with everyone. It has become an equalizer for him among his peers. It gives him something to talk about and share with them to help him make new friends. The joy of this book came because Nathan isn't shy about sharing who he is. He is not ashamed or embarrassed by his condition. He has turned this difficult situation into something that can bless anyone who comes in contact with him. Because of this, he has really spread his wings and is flying.

This was not the end of Nathan's book. The success of Dallas's vision expanded and Flying Bobcat Theater Company and The Salt Lake Acting Company came together and created a beautiful play based on his story. The adaptation to the theater was beautiful. The vision of bringing these birds to life was mesmerizing. The Salt Lake Acting Company ran the play for the whole month of March in 2016. Joy filled us from Nathan's touching people's lives with his story and not hiding from pain or discomfort. He attended many of the performances with broken arms but never with a broken smile. March was a month of pure joy for our family. We attended over twenty of the performances. Nathan signed lots of playbills and was even able to bring his third-grade class on a field trip to see the play. After they saw it, they made amazing thank-you cards, and the lobby was decorated in drawings these eight- and nine-year-olds had created. As Nathan always says, it was *the best day ever*!

Nathan once had a terrible fall that reminded us just how fragile life is. Falls for an OI child can be deadly, and Nathan is no different. While in a grocery store parking lot, I was loading the car. I went to take off Nathan's chest harness, not realizing his lap belt was undone as well. Nathan leaned forward to play with a toy but kept going and fell out of the chair and smacked his head on the pavement. That sound, similar to an egg being dropped, will forever be in my mind. Instinctively, I scooped him up and almost panicked. If his neck broke, I shouldn't have moved him. Already in my arms, though, I placed him in the closest car seat. It wasn't until later that I realized it was Jason's seat and not his. Nathan was screaming in pain, and tears fogged my glasses. I knew I could not make it all the way to the hospital, so I drove a couple miles to Ryan's work. I quickly called him, and he met me outside with his dad, who he works for. They gave Nathan a blessing, and Ryan then drove us to the hospital. Nathan's whole right side was broken—arm, leg, and ribs—and his left arm was broken too. The biggest concern was the skull fracture that extended from his eye socket all the way to the back of his head and the epidural hematoma forming at the fracture. The doctors took many CT scans, and we spent four days in the ICU not knowing if each would be the last day we would have with him. Family and friends cared for Jason and Courtney, and we had support and prayers for Nathan all over. He pulled through, the bleed was absorbed naturally, and there was no need for surgery.

We met Dr. Brockmeyer at this time. He is a neurosurgeon and was following Nathan's injury and noticed what is called basilar invagination (BI). This was the first time we were alerted to this serious condition. It basically meant the bones of Nathan's neck could not hold up his head, so his head fell onto the spine. This can cause the spinal cord to become pinched. Dr. Brockmeyer started following Nathan with regular MRIs to watch the progression of his BI. It held stable for several years.

In August 2016, Nathan had another fall. We were at a water park getting ready to go home, and thinking Nathan was all buckled, I pushed him down the parking lot ramp, where he fell out of his chair. Memories of the previous fall flashed back. Nathan, being stronger, however, was able to twist around and land on his shoulder and then his head. We had a friend help us give Nathan a blessing, and we rushed him to the emergency room. After scans and x-rays, we found that he did have a small skull fracture but no bleed. His arm and ribs were broken too. We stayed overnight for observation but were sent home quickly this time.

In October 2016, we were getting Nathan ready for a rod replacement surgery. He had outgrown the rod in his tibia, and his bone was starting to curve below the rod. Because of Nathan's BI, Dr. Brockmeyer told us to have any doctors contact him before surgery. Due to the risk to his spinal cord, intubation could be difficult, even deadly. The doctor wanted to talk with the anesthesiologists to help them know what they were dealing with. Dr. Brockmeyer had approved several successful surgeries since Nathan's BI diagnosis, so we thought this was going to be another run-of-the-mill surgery and he would be recovering in no time. The CT scan from August's fall showed a whole different story. Dr. Brockmeyer contacted us the week of Nathan's scheduled rodding surgery and told us his BI had progressed to the point that he could not recommend any surgeries without stabilizing his neck first. The risk of his spinal cord becoming pinched or even severed was too great.

Dr. Brockmeyer was surprised to learn Nathan didn't have any symptoms of his cord being pinched as it was. He said we could wait for symptoms, but we couldn't perform any other surgeries while we waited. The symptoms we would be looking for would be trouble breathing, tingling in the arms, trouble swallowing—things we were not comfortable seeing.

As a rock settled into Ryan's, Nathan's, and my hearts, we decided we needed to do the surgery as soon as possible so we could get back to living. This was the surgery we had been dreading for years, since his first fall. To correct his BI, surgeons would have to fuse the skull in place, hopefully only fusing the c-spine. They would surgically insert rods held by screws into his skull and vertebrae. They would also pack it with cadaver bone and a chemical designed to stimulate the bone fusion process. He would then wear a custom collar and wait for the bone to fuse.

Ryan and I were beside ourselves. How could they do this with Nathan's quality of bone? Just knowing the difficulty we'd had getting rods into his long bones that are not screwed into the bone made it all too clear that this would be an extreme challenge.

Nathan, nervous, still found a way to smile. In our discussions with the doctor, it sounded like he would have to fuse further down in Nathan's spine to find stable enough vertebrae to screw into. This would mean he would lose any motion in his neck. This really scared Nathan. Knowing this would most likely happen, we reached out to a friend who, as a teenager, had had to have his neck fused. Now in college, he came over and talked to Nathan. Nathan could see how happy and full his life was, and it helped us all feel ready to go get it done and over with.

I felt all alone and scared. Nathan is my whole world, inasmuch as I care for him day in and day out. He is the one we as a family rally around; he's the one who has glued us together. My children mean everything to me, but Nathan is the one who needs me most. In a sense, caring for him has defined me, my family, and our journey. Take that away and I am not sure I would survive.

This was so scary for me. My light started dimming. I should have reached out and asked for help, especially from my Heavenly Father! But I didn't. I retreated into myself. I was just going through the motions and trying not to feel. All I wanted to do between the news of the surgery and the actual surgery was gather my kids around me and play and watch movies and let the world disappear. But while fun and memorable, I was not allowing myself to feel what I needed to feel.

We had our family pictures taken. Nathan wanted to make sure he was not in the collar for his picture that year. I could not bring myself to say it, but I was scared to my core that I was losing my baby, my life, my world, and I kept it inside. The adversary was working hard on me.

The six-hour-long surgery took place on October 17, 2016, after which, Nathan was taken to the ICU with the breathing tube still in. He was miserable. He hurt and couldn't talk or move, and my heart broke to see him so unhappy. Recovery continued, tubes and wires were removed, and a collar was fitted. The whole time, Nathan was not feeling well. Sitting was excruciating. This was the first time the spark that he carried was not as bright. It worried me, but he was still here, and we were determined to get through this. Nathan and I stayed in the hospital for six days, and we were able to take him home in a rear-facing car seat that allowed him to only have to sit up at forty-five degrees. A good friend bought us a yard lounge chair that could be lowered and raised as Nathan needed. We padded it, and this became his spot.

At about three weeks, we went in to see if the stitches could be removed and to look at a spot on his head that was not healing. Because Nathan could not sit and was constantly lying on his incision so the collar was applying pressure there, the wound was not healing properly. While in the doctor's office, we got x-rays that Nathan had to sit up for, which was not easy or comfortable at the time. The x-ray revealed that the screws in his skull had come out. This made sense as to why he was having so much pain. Now we needed to start over! Absolutely devastated, we scheduled the second surgery. Nathan broke down in the doctor's office. I told him it was okay to cry, it didn't make him any less brave, and sometimes you just need to let it out.

Dr. Brockmeyer was so sweet with him. He told him he did not need to worry, that Mommy and Daddy could worry a little but that he (the doctor) was going to worry the most, so Nathan did not need to. This time, I reached out and asked for some divine help. I got a blessing, and this really helped calm my soul as we went into this second surgery. I was still feeling lost and alone but more at peace.

For this surgery, they put in a system that would sandwich the bone instead of screwing into the bone. The recovery was still five days in the hospital, but they double-checked everything before they released us to make sure it was holding. We also had plastic surgery involved to help close the incision due to the healing issues with his skin.

We had him sitting up soon after and felt better about this surgery. We went on with life for four months. He was ready to go in for the CT scan to see how the fusion was going. Life was back to a new normal. He was back to school and getting around on his own. I was back to work, and we were grateful.

When we went in for the scan, we received heartbreaking news. The fusion was good from T4–C3, but the bone at C3—the skull—had disappeared. The theory was that instead of becoming bone, the body created scar tissue. Nathan needed another surgery, which we set for the end of March.

For the next month, we struggled with loosening hardware and stabilization. The hardware ended up needing to be completely removed, and he was placed in a halo. The next nine months were extremely difficult. Nathan had to be on a strong antibiotic administered through a central line. Going anywhere was nearly impossible. He also started home hospital schooling through our district.

Slowly, he regained his strength and then some. As it neared the time for the halo to be removed, Nathan was sitting up on his own and even starting to figure out how to scoot around. His resilience and desire to never give up kept us going. Watching him find joy while in what he called a torture device was simply a miracle. And as he improved, he received the opportunity to fly to New York City to see the Yankees play. He was also able to give speeches and encourage others to never give up.

This part of his story is still being written. While as a family we prayed and hoped this would be the ending of this phase and Nathan would have a full recovery, that was not in the Lord's plan. At the time of the writing, we were informed that Nathan's spinal cord was still in a compromising position and that there may even be evidence of spinal cord damage occurring, but he still wasn't presenting outward symptoms; we as a family went home and fasted and prayed.

Nathan is not ready to give up. He wants to try again, knowing this means more painful surgeries, more hardware, possibly another halo. As parents, my husband and I agreed that if he is willing to go for it, we will support him all the way. Hardware is being designed and made specifically to fit Nathan. We continue to press forward with faith. The Lord knows our hearts and hears our prayers; we have witnessed it and have no doubt He will again.

And we have no doubt Nathan will carry his smile with him through the remainder of his journey. He is a source of joy to all who meet him!

Starting with his first surgery, Nathan started giving out chocolate to all who visited him—nurses, friends, and doctors. At his last surgery, he was able to get in his wheelchair and deliver little chocolate kisses to everyone. His joy for life is infectious and even at his lowest, Nathan always seems to choose sharing joy.

PART V: MISSIONS

Chapter 9
Called to Serve: Mission and Mental Illness
By Tylyn Adams

When I was a junior in high school, I felt lost and alone. I had friends, but I never felt like they really cared about me. I was someone they kept around, but I wasn't worth spending time with outside of school. I felt like I couldn't talk to anyone about the situation, so I hid it. I did my best to fake being happy. I got caught up in self-harm. It was the only release I found. Things got worse and worse, and I started thinking about suicide. It scared me to have those thoughts, but it also seemed like it was the best option.

That February, I went to the Sweethearts dance. It was the first time I had genuine fun in months. It was when I realized I could still be happy and enjoy my life. It pushed me to tell my family about the self-harm. Telling my parents was one of the hardest things I'd ever done. I felt like I had failed them and had caused them unnecessary pain and sadness. It was horrible.

* * *

I started my mission papers in October 2016. I had it all planned out. I'd work full-time until I left on my mission, I would leave in February right after I turned nineteen, I would have the greatest time, and then I would come home and have my life figured out. I was so excited because this felt like I was beginning a new life: my transition from high school to being an adult. But nothing really went the way I had planned. Because I had a history with self-harm and never actually received professional help for it, there were a lot of steps I had to take before submitting my papers.

I started seeing a counselor in December 2016, even though I didn't think I needed to talk to anyone. At this point, it had been over a year and a half since I had last hurt myself. I thought I was healed. My counselor said she would clear me to serve a mission, but she still wanted to meet with me until I left. These sessions were when I realized how much guilt and shame I still felt. I was ashamed of myself for hurting or ruining my body. I felt as if I had failed God. He had given me so many things, but I had messed it all up. All the thoughts I had about my self-harm were negative, and I was afraid of what people would think of me. If they knew how I had failed in the past, they would pity me.

I'd done a lot of online reading that convinced me the scars weren't attractive and that my husband wouldn't like them. I read that my children would think I was weak because of the scars. For over two years, that was how I saw what had happened.

My counselor was the first person I told about my scars, and she said it was okay. She never saw them, but she talked me through coping skills I knew could help me and ones I could improve on. Honestly, what helped me the most was photography. I love taking and editing pictures, and that became my happy place, my outlet. My joy.

By the end of December, I met with my stake president, and he was going to submit my papers, or so I thought. Four weeks went by, and I thought I was going to get my mission call. I was so excited. On Monday, I got a text from my bishop, asking if I could meet with him. I knew something was wrong. I met with him and found out there had been a miscommunication between the stake president and bishop, and my papers had never actually been submitted. I was so crushed and confused.

I was praying, reading my scriptures, serving in my ward, doing all the things I needed to do to show God I was serious. But one thing after another kept going wrong. I didn't get it. I wanted to do something good. I wanted to serve my Lord full-time. Why was it so hard for me to do something righteous? Was it not what He wanted from me?

That night, I went home and cried. I didn't know what to think, so I dropped to my knees and prayed. I told Him how disappointed and frustrated I was. That I wanted to serve a mission but was it not what He wanted for me? Was this a sign that I shouldn't go?

And as soon as I thought that, the impression came to keep trying. The Spirit prompted that this was for a reason and that I just needed to keep pushing. I asked God to help me. Help me not be angry. I asked for enough faith to keep going. And then I got up and kept going.

I really tried my best to keep a good attitude and to not get bitter over the wait. I trusted and did my best to learn and grow from it. I listened to

Elder Dieter F. Uchtdorf's talk "The Infinite Power of Hope" every day for months. His words reminded me that I needed to put my hope in Christ and work. So I did.

I tried my best to improve myself and grow closer to Christ and Heavenly Father. That time was when I relied on God more than I ever had in the past. I threw away my plan and just worked to know what He wanted me to do and what He wanted me to learn.

* * *

On February 16, 2017, I was called to serve and labor in the Texas Fort Worth Mission, Spanish speaking. I couldn't believe it. I was finally going to serve a full-time mission. I naively believed that after I got my call, everything would be perfect. I'd go to the MTC and then straight to Texas. As far as I was concerned, my emotional health issues were gone, and I had been healed from my past.

I reported to the Provo MTC on April 19. What a week that was. Before going into the MTC, I wondered what I was getting myself into. The anxiety was overwhelming as I thought of leaving everyone I loved and going to do something completely new and foreign. I cried so much that first week. I felt so guilty leaving my family; I felt like they needed me home more than I needed to serve a mission. Honestly, I cried so much that my first Saturday, I told one of the sister training leaders that I needed to go home. I was done. I thought she was going to try to talk me out of it or say anything other than what she did. She told me that if I felt like I needed to go home, I should go home. She asked me to wait and talk to our branch president about it on Sunday and to try it out for little bit longer. Then we lay on her bed together and cried and ate food. She too was having a really hard time in the MTC, and we connected so easily.

The next day, I talked to my branch president about how I was feeling and asked him to give me a priesthood blessing. I immediately felt better. It was confirmed to me that I was where I needed to be, that my family would be okay, and that I needed to focus on what I wanted to do. After that, I felt great. I knew I was where I needed to be. I started connecting with my district, especially the sisters.

I really could not have done those first weeks in the MTC without the elders and sisters in my district and zone. As soon as I felt things improve, things just got harder. Over the next two weeks, my old thoughts of self-harm came back but this time worse than they had been before.

I recognized the feeling and immediately told my sister training leaders about it. I talked to them a lot throughout my struggles, and we really worked to get me to stop having those feelings. I prayed, I ran, and I worked. I did as much as I could to try to make myself forget the thoughts. But two weeks went by, and it was only getting worse, so we decided it was time I talked to one of the MTC counselors.

Going into it, I thought the counselor would just listen to me, give me a little advice, tell me to try harder, and send me on my way. What I thought was going to take an hour ended up taking five hours. I was honest with her about everything—my history with feelings of self-harm, my depression, and my anxiety. After awhile, she suggested that I start taking antidepressants, and that was the point where I completely lost it. I was crying as I tried to deny that I needed medicine, that I wasn't that far gone that I needed to be medicated to get through the day. The therapist and I talked for a long time about it, how going on medicine for mental issues wasn't giving up. For some people, it was the last piece of the puzzle.

After my appointment, my companion and I went over and talked to one of the MTC doctors. I told him what my counselor and I had talked about, and he asked me if I had any other questions or concerns about it. All I could think of were characters in TV shows who had taken mental medicine. They always said how they don't feel like themselves on it. I told him of my fear, and he asked me if I felt like myself right now. Here I was, a nineteen-year-old girl who had cried every night for the past two and a half weeks, couldn't concentrate on anything, and sat in front of this doctor, still crying my eyes out. I realized then that this wasn't how it was supposed to be. I didn't deserve to be miserable; I didn't need to be distracted all the time; I didn't need to always be sad. So I started taking the medication. I was asked three times that day if I wanted to go home. I knew before they even finished the sentence that I didn't. I needed to stay.

I was extremely blessed to have an amazing companion during this time. Honestly, I really struggled being with her in the beginning. She was always so happy and goofy. I didn't understand how someone could be that happy and excited about literally everything. But that day, I opened up and told her everything that was going on. I told her how scared I felt, and she was there for me. She hadn't had any other experiences with people with mental illnesses, but she did her best to talk to me and respect what I was doing. She was a blessing.

That night, my branch president came over to see how I was doing. He had talked to the counselor about everything and was worried about me. Being able to talk to him helped me so much. It was nice to have a parental figure telling me it was okay.

At this point, I told my district and the branch president what was going on. I couldn't believe how positive and supporting they all were. A lot of the sisters in my district said they had a family member or that they personally had taken medicine to help with mental health issues at one point or another. They showed me so much love during this time—and that brought joy during an emotional storm. During a time when I felt horrible about myself, I was shown the most love I had ever been given.

Over the next couple weeks, I met with my counselor twice a week, and we worked a lot on me owning my story. Accepting my past and using it as an experience to help others rather than looking at it as something shameful that should always stay hidden. The counseling, along with some amazing missionaries, helped me to accept my past. I began to love where I came from rather than hide from it.

There was a sister in my district who would always tell me it was okay to have a bad day or even a bad week. We talked about how things might still be hard but that I could push forward and recognize my feelings rather than hide them. I showed her my scars. She was the first person I showed my scars to, and it was extremely hard for me. But I did it and told her intimate stories about each of them, stories that almost no one knew. And it was the first time I didn't feel disgusted by my body. I wasn't ashamed of how I looked. I had come to accept myself enough to show even one person my scars.

It took awhile to figure out the right medication levels. They put me on a long-term and short-term medicine. I was just going to take the short-term one until the long-term one started to kick in, so after a few weeks, I stopped taking the short-term medicine. Within a day, I started having a lot of anxiety and disturbing thoughts. I struggled a lot that day. I was trying my hardest to understand and speak Spanish, but it was too much with all the thoughts I was having. For most of that lesson, I relied on what the Spirit told me to say. It ended up being our most powerful lesson; the Spirit was so strong. The thoughts resumed after the lesson, and I was really stressed out because I wasn't supposed to have those kinds of thoughts and feelings. I was serving a mission. I told one of my best friends in my district, and she told me to just wait until my appointment the next day with the counselor and talk to her about it.

At my appointment, I shared everything that had happened after going off the short-term medicine. We had a long talk about those thoughts and feelings and my history with them. At the end, she diagnosed me with OCD, which took me by surprise because I didn't have the physical signs of OCD. I didn't realize OCD was more than flicking on and off a light switch or constantly washing my hands. Both my counselor and doctor decided it was best if I switched to taking Prozac because it was more effective in treating OCD.

* * *

I switched medicines a week before I was supposed to leave for the mission field. They told me I was going to be extended two weeks, and an hour later, I got my flight plans. Everyone was so excited about finally being able to leave the MTC, to go out and serve, to do what we had all been waiting to do. Again, it felt like I had failed. I had been trying my best to follow what the Lord wanted, and here was another setback.

I was so scared to stay in the MTC another two weeks. Staying meant that I would join another district in my zone and become a trio. I was so close to my first district, and I thought I would get seventh wheeled in the second one. I was now that weird kid—the missionary who was having problems and had to stay.

That next week, on Saturday, which was my p-day in the MTC, we went to an early-morning session in the temple. That morning had been stressful, but getting to the temple was such a breath of fresh air. After the session had finished, we were all in the celestial room, and I noticed a couple sitting on the couches, just crying. I felt so drawn to them. I had never talked to them, but I felt so much love for them, and I wanted to help them, but I didn't because I thought it wouldn't be appropriate for where we were.

My companion and I went to the dressing room, and I was waiting for her when I saw the wife from the celestial room. I thought it'd be super weird, but I went for it and asked her if I could give her a hug. She said yes and told me how her son had just recently died. Honestly, I didn't know what to do in that moment. I just hugged her and told her that her son was okay and that she and her family could get through this. We talked for about five minutes, but that experience stayed with me. I hoped and prayed that she was doing well.

Sunday was a really big day for me. I was expecting to have a hard day. It was my last Sunday with my district; the sister I had shown my scars to was leaving at 3 a.m. on Monday. Instead of being miserable, it was the first day in I don't even know how long that I was genuinely happy all day. It was so cool; I was so excited. Sundays were always the best because it was when my district and zone would just have fun. Yes, we studied a little in the morning and went to church, but with the temple walk and choir, we just had fun.

Over the next two days, everyone from my first district left for their mission fields. I had never seen more joy in someone's face than I did when my sisters and elders left for their areas. I was there to drop off almost all of them, and it was such a spiritual experience.

Tuesday was the last day with one of the sisters, whom I had become good friends with, and two of the elders. Tuesday night was when it all hit me. My MTC family was leaving. That night as the four of us walked back to our dorms, we were saying our goodbyes, and it hit me that I wasn't going to see them again for at least another year and a half to two years. I started to cry, and then one of the elders from my new district shook my hand and told me he loved me. That was the moment I lost it.

The sister and I went back to our room and made a plan. When I found out that it was just going to be the two of us in the room for the night, I came up with a going-away "gift" for her. We used all the sheets and blankets from the beds, pulled two of the mattresses onto the floor, and built a fort. It was one of the greatest nights of my life. We ate tons of junk food, talked about what we loved and what we hated, and just talked about everything. It was like I was having a sleepover in the MTC. It was the best.

The next morning, I dropped her off at the travel office, went back to the dorms, and joined my new room, which included my trio and another companionship. Within the first few hours of being in that new district, I knew that was where I needed to be. The two weeks I was in that district were the best two weeks of my life. Hermana Hardin, who was part of my new companionship, and I immediately clicked. I knew I could be open and honest with her and she would help me the best way she could. We would make eye contact and make each other laugh, which happened a few times at very inappropriate times. Even when I was having a bad day, I knew I could be around her and feel better.

I know now that I needed those people in my life. I was so happy and learned so much during those extra two weeks. They had this uniqueness about them that allowed them to have fun and still invite the Spirit. On one of the p-days, we celebrated an elder's birthday. We bought him knee-length fashion socks he was really going to need in cold Costa Rica and sent him a Dear Elder of brownies that we ate during the Sunday night movie. Those additional days in the MTC brought more love and joy into my life. There are very few things I love more than the missionaries from my "extra" district.

* * *

During my last week in the MTC, I developed a tremor. They thought it was just a side effect of the Prozac, but my MTC doctor wanted someone to be able to watch the tremor closer than they could from the mission field. With less than a week before I was supposed to go to the mission field, I was told I was going to be sent home. Another broken heart. I was back to being confused. Even though I was in the best spiritual, mental, and physical shape of my life, I was being sent home. Hermana Hardin wasn't a really touchy-feely person, but after I told my companions I was going home, she held my hand for hours. I never knew how comforting it could be to just hold someone's hand.

We went from the doctors to our classroom; luckily, we passed only one person from our zone, and he didn't ask why I was crying. We got to our class, and two of our elders were there. I asked one of them to give me a blessing and told them what had happened. He gave me a blessing, and we left again to talk to our district president. We talked about me going home and called my parents. It was a weird feeling because there was still a slim chance I could stay, but I knew I was likely going home. It was hard. I prayed and prayed to be able to trust in God and His plan. One of the elders told me about a trial his family had passed through. At first, they had prayed to be able to overcome the trial. But things had worsened, so instead of praying for improvement, they had started praying that they would have the faith to endure the trial.

I reflected on that story a lot. On the days when I just wanted to be healed and have everything go my way, I realized I wouldn't learn anything. Without having my faith tested, I would not experience growth. Whenever I felt discouraged or upset, I remembered those the Lord had blessed me with, and I felt better. I felt my pain swallowed up in joy.

* * *

Soon after I came home, the tremor went away. Within a few days, I was cleared by my doctor and counselor to return to the mission field, though

I didn't return for another four months. It was hard coming home. I still felt like somewhere along the way I had messed up. I did my best to push away those feelings and focus on the good—on the lessons I had learned in those final weeks in the MTC. Part of the plan was enduring to the end, and sometimes that was giving up what my plan was and walking by faith. I really relied on the experiences I had had with my fellow companions.

When I first got home, I felt like there was something here I needed to find, some bigger reason that I had come home. After being home for a couple weeks, I ran into Ganel-Lyn. She and her husband used to be my Sunday School teachers. I tried so hard to get them to forget I existed, but they didn't, even though I was one of those annoying teenagers who had pushed them away every chance I'd had. They had never given up on me. It made me so happy to see them and talk with them. That was when Ganel-Lyn asked me to write my story for her new book.

I thought, *What? How cool is that?*

The Condies also asked if I would share everything I had experienced with the stake mission prep class they taught. I was nervous, but I said yes. I had already decided I wasn't going to hide behind fear or shame anymore. I was going to embrace who I was.

That had come step by step. First, I had felt prompted to tell one of the elders in my district. I was still afraid to tell people, but I was learning to follow promptings. Second was when I spoke to the stake mission prep group. I shared with the soon-to-be-missionaries that sometimes things are hard in the MTC. I opened up about how my entire mission process had been difficult. It had tested my faith—more than I thought possible, but it had been one of the happiest and most rewarding times of my life. My MTC experience didn't go how I thought it would, and that was okay. I met so many amazing people and grew closer to my Father in Heaven. It was then that I truly developed my own relationship with God and converted myself to Christ.

Finally, and probably my favorite part of coming home early related to the sister in the celestial room, Stephanie. When I met her in the temple, she had just lost her son. After I spoke to the stake mission prep class, Ganel-Lyn posted a picture of me on Facebook. As only God could orchestrate, Stephanie and Ganel-Lyn were friends. From Ganel-Lyn's post, Stephanie recognized me as the sister in the temple. She and I were able to talk. I was so grateful we were able to find each other again. I had thought about her, her family, and her son so many times. I had a cousin who died last year, and

Stephanie's son was only a few years older than my cousin when she died. I felt so drawn to Stephanie. And now, because I was sent home with the tremor, we are connected beyond a hug and a conversation in the temple. I'm so grateful to have Stephanie's example in my life.

* * *

There's a constant feeling that I'm still trying to go on my mission. And then one thing after another stops it from happening. Sometimes I get discouraged and wonder why this is all happening. I wonder if I'm not doing enough. But then I attend the temple, read my scriptures, or attend church, and when I'm able to feel the Spirit, I'm reminded of whose hands I'm in, and my pain is swallowed up in His joy.

I have had the strongest spiritual experiences of my life in the temple since coming home. I can easily focus on the little things that go wrong, but for the most part, they are the things I can't control. If I take a step back, I see all the good. Over the last ten months, I have grown so much. I'm so grateful for those experiences of sorrow and frustration because of the increased growth and joy that has come into my life.

As of this writing, I'm back out on my mission. I know this is what I needed. And I know it's what my family needed. I have been *called to serve* both at home and in Texas. And no matter where I go, I choose faith, growth, and joy over old shame.

Chapter 10
My Fairy Tale: Single in Hollywood
By Kristen Metzger

ONCE UPON A TIME, A boy broke a girl's heart.

This girl had never seen her heart in so many pieces. Her heart like shattered glass, she wondered if she would ever be able to mend every shard and sliver back into one whole heart.

Where was her fairy godmother?

However, a fairy's magic would not run deep enough for matters of the heart.

The girl turned to her Heavenly Father. "Please, hold my heart. Hold it together so it can continue to beat until it is strong enough to beat alone."

And He did. He held her heart and her hand as she struggled to navigate the world with a distorted lens of the way things were. The boy had made her view of men foggy and unforgiving. She assumed the worst from the start, and with each disappointment, her fears were confirmed. The tears would come, and the anger would simmer.

"How could you leave me in this single world?" she would scream in her mind, hoping the boy would hear her thoughts across the miles.

But he was happily married, with no scars to remind him of the girl who had seemed so easily disposable.

She did not recognize herself anymore. These negative feelings were strangers in her normally hopeful disposition.

Her initial fear was that her heart would harden in its defensive response, making it impossible to heal or mend. She prayed for divine help to keep her heart soft yet strong.

Miraculously, she was surrounded by people who needed her love and who had such great love to return. It was difficult for a heart to harden when it was actively loving and receiving love.

Her heart stayed soft and slowly but surely regained its strength. This muscle for love stretched and gave and grew in return. This was no magic from the wand of a fairy godmother but was the power and reality of charity, the pure love of Christ.

This is my fairy tale. Where is the "happily ever after," you ask? Well, if by that you mean, did she find her Prince Charming . . . no, I have not. But the magic of this fairy tale is that the "happily ever after" has already begun—the "happily ever after" that will sustain this pending princess across the miles, heartaches, dragon fights, and lonely moments in her tower. This damsel may have moments of distress, but she has found the strength to choose joy, with or without a prince to save her.

I am a thirty-one-year-old lady-in-waiting. I am a member of The Church of Jesus Christ. I am still single. What could that look like? Rejection. What could that feel like? Lonely. Frustrating.

I have been pursuing acting professionally in Los Angeles for the last three years. What could that look like? Rejection. What could that feel like? Lonely. Frustrating.

This is perhaps all the world might choose to see. I run toward the red carpet, tripping over disappointments with boys and auditions, losing every glass slipper I offer in hopes that either my prince will find it or an incredible director will realize I am the perfect fit for his leading lady. So far, one would think I am just out a number of expensive and delicate glass slippers. But there is so much more to this story! Around every corner of disappointment, there are moments of delight and triumph. Beyond every frustrating date is a new friend or a good story. Within reach of each lonely night is an overwhelming abundance of love waiting to be shared. The harder the journey, the greater the opportunity for God to show His handiwork. There is space for miracles and joy. And I see them everywhere.

I remember a day when I needed reassurance regarding my purpose in Los Angeles. I went to the temple with a prayer for confirmation to continue my journey on the red carpet or for instructions to change directions. I felt peace in the temple, and as I walked out, I was alerted to a new voicemail on my phone. It was a casting director for a commercial. He wanted to Skype-audition with me that evening for a shoot the next day. The audition was fun, and they were so complimentary as they decided in the moment to cast me! This commercial did not catapult my career, but it was a gratefully received answer to prayer.

I remember meeting a boy at a Halloween Harry Potter–themed party. He was so kind and fun. We exchanged numbers so we could share photos from that evening. A few days later, I had a sweet friend struggling deeply with emotions of inadequacy just moments before needing to board a flight to Australia for her mission. The guy I'd met at the party worked by the airport, and I texted him to ask if he could come give her a blessing. He left work early and gave her a blessing that was so clearly from her Heavenly Father. We all felt great love and peace. I treated him to Chipotle in sincere gratitude. We might have had a third wheel on that "date," but it too was an answer to prayer. I had been praying to find men who were kind, loved the Lord, and respected their priesthood. Check, check, check.

I chose this path. And I must choose how to live on it and what to see. It is a thrilling path filled with spotlights, Mutual dates, and chocolate, oh my. (*All* dark chocolate.) It is an adventure for which I sought wisdom from my experience as a full-time missionary.

In 2007, I was called to serve in the Nauvoo Illinois Mission. With that calling came great responsibility. It was a hard eighteen months. It was also the most glorious and fulfilling eighteen months. Why? Because for those many months, I knew what my purpose was and that God was with me every step of the way. This was for Him, for His children. I could do anything and everything—no matter the cost. I was exhausted and happy beyond measure. I was with God, joyfully serving. And I served "happily ever after."

After coming home, I knew I had to continue to serve "happily ever after"; I had to uphold that seemingly climactic experience of serving as a full-time representative of Jesus Christ. I had to figure out how to return to the "real world" and be happy.

I decided my career goals in acting would be my next "mission," so the hashtag for my Hollywood chapter became #calledtoserveinlosangeles. It was my call to serve and be a light for the Lord in a city of temptations and deceptions. Many people warned me of this danger before I left for LA. But with each powerful film I watched, I would creep to the edge of my seat with glistening eyes, feeling my heart tugged in the direction of the West Coast. This is often how I receive guidance from the Lord; I feel the fire blowing in a certain direction. And when I took that inspired desire to the Lord, I saw the green light. I packed my car and headed as far west as I could go.

Each audition and every day on set became an opportunity to lift those around me who were in the same gloriously frustrating boat as me: a twenty- to thirty-something-year-old girl chasing her dream to be a Hollywood actress. I saw reminders of this beneath my feet and all around me. Every time I didn't get a part, it was an opportunity to fall on my knees and feel hope in the One I trusted.

Just a few months after I arrived in LA, I was invited to audition for a girls' a cappella group called the Lolas. My beatboxing skills and capacity to sing lower than most women sealed the deal. Every girl's group needs a good bass. These girls became some of my dearest friends. It was refreshing to meet together each week and unite our voices in interesting harmonies and sounds. It became a grounding gift for me as an artist in a sea of shifting auditions and gigs. Then the opportunity deepened. Each time we went out after a show, the girls would laugh in good cheer as the sole virgin in the group (me) ordered her ginger beer, and the questions came. As their respect for my beliefs grew, the questions became more sincere and of greater significance. At our retreats, we would clutch pillows and talk about the purpose of this life, the eternal nature of families, and the power of prayer with a Father in Heaven who loves us.

Equally so, I had the opportunity to grow in my dating life. Every time another boy disappointed or just wasn't the best match for me, it was an opportunity to fall on my knees and feel hope in the One I trusted. With full purpose of heart and God at my side, Hollywood became a home for my refining. I found so many who needed the strength of my heart. I met one boy outside a little café in Echo Park before he went on to perform with his band. I stayed for his show, and we ended up going on a few dates. I loved his fresh perspective, and he was learning what it looked like to date a Mormon girl who chose to live the law of chastity. We became good friends.

The morning after his father passed away unexpectedly happened to be a day we had planned to do breakfast. When I got to his house, he introduced me to his sister as his "Mormon friend here to comfort him." I think we were both grateful that day to be together, despite our different lifestyles and beliefs that kept any romantic relationship from progressing. He, for the confirmation of a truth he hoped for—to see his father again. And me? My heart seemed to garner greater strength in the arms of someone who needed it even more than I did.

And yet, there were days when my heart felt weak and tired.

I found great solace and purpose in yet another hashtag of truth: #lovethewaiting. I would choose to love the moments between dreams. These moments were and continue to be precious opportunities to see God working.

The journey between dreams, the time between one answered prayer and the next answered prayer was where the best magic happens, for this was the time and the means allotted for me to become like our Heavenly Father.

A few months after, I moved to Los Angeles. I noticed a guy in my ward who made very thoughtful and deep comments in Sunday School. He had a long blonde ponytail and looked very strong. Thor? Shortly after we met, I was given an opportunity to invite a man I would like to date to interview for a new dating show with me. Naturally, I invited him. We didn't know each other very well, but he was up for the adventure. We didn't end up getting cast on the show, but that was the start of a wonderful friendship. I wondered if he could be the best match for me.

Flash forward a number of months when he married his best match, another dear friend of mine in the ward. I love these two together. Going to their sealing was a sweet honor. I wrote in my journal: "The sealer spoke of the love that brought everyone in the room together—the love of Jake and Michelle and the love everyone has for the two of them! The energy in the room fueled by love so real and palpable—ah, love!"

Did my heart feel tempted to engage in a pity party? Of course. But thankfully, our agency is a strong gift, and I just can't deny the fruits of love! It is contagious. Thus, I choose joy. It is remarkably refreshing. And each time I go to yet another sealing or wedding of two friends who are getting married "before me," I am in awe of the opportunity to be taught by the Spirit of the eternities this great plan of happiness and to see my heart growing and softening with hope. Yes, every rose has its thorns. The temptations can be distracting, but the journey is a beautiful one if we choose for it to be.

* * *

My greatest temptations are not as easily seen as others'. They are deeply internal.

Anxiety. Will I get enough acting gigs to pay rent? Will I be in the right place at the right time? To meet the right guy? To make the right industry connections?

Frustration. If I am supposed to be on this path, why is it so hard? Aren't my desires righteous?

Doubt. Am I good enough? Am I desirable enough? Am I kidding myself? Did I really feel prompted to follow this dream?

Self-Pity. It is never my turn. I am stuck. I have no control over my dreams.

Jealousy/Comparison. Why does it seem so easy for her? Where are her trials?

These temptations are real. The thinking errors are deceptively and carefully carved into my heart. Those tears in my eyes are real. I shared this on social media one difficult day, with a photo of a teary-eyed-me pressing a phone to my ear: "Heaven knows we need never be ashamed of our tears, for they are rain upon the blinding dust of the earth, overlying our hard hearts. I was better after I had cried, than before—more sorry, more aware of my own ingratitude, more gentle."—Charles Dickens. ***This phone call was heaven-sent to a little girl who needed to remember who she is, what she has been given, and where she can go. #regroundedingratitude #freedomtochange #freedomtochoose"

My mama was just a phone call away. My Father in Heaven is just a prayer away. He knows my heart. And with Him, I can emerge triumphant from my moments of weakness and heartache—not just okay but gloriously more capable of giving!

"And it came to pass that the Lord did visit them with his Spirit, and said unto them: Be comforted. And they were comforted. And the Lord said unto them also: Go forth among the Lamanites, thy brethren, and establish my word; yet ye shall be patient in long-suffering and afflictions, that ye may show forth good examples unto them in me, and I will make an instrument of thee in my hands unto the salvation of many souls."[33]

Amen! I will gladly press on in this simultaneously exhausting and exhilarating journey if I can be an instrument in the Lord's hands! There is no place I would rather be. I know I must rise up in the midst of trials and heartaches, for that is how I will be refined and enabled to empathize with more of God's children. This is a choice I must make in every moment. In the eye of the storm, we will find calm if we choose love. As I continue to run toward two dreams that could seem to get farther and farther away, I have added this mantra to my daily agenda: "Choose love." Regardless of the number of casting directors I don't hear back from or the number of men who don't call, the power is still in my hands. In a world where I could play the damsel in distress, I can wield the sword of truth and be a superhero instead.

I learned what my superpower would be when I went to the islands of Fiji. Because Heavenly Father knows His nomadic daughter, He opened

---

33 Alma 17:10–11.

a door for me to get involved with HEFY (Humanitarian Experience for Youth). In the summer of 2016, I was graciously given the opportunity to serve as a trip leader for two groups of twenty LDS youth for four weeks in Fiji. We spent our days digging large holes and mixing and pouring cement to build bathrooms for families in very poor villages. We spent our evenings loving and learning with the youth in the local wards. I remember one Sunday feeling overwhelmed by the amount of love I was feeling for my kids, the families in the village, and the sweet ward members.

It was so tangible, I secretly worried that I might explode. Was this what a pending heart attack felt like? I offered a prayer, asking what I should do with this love when it felt I was already giving as much as I imagined I could.

This was my answer: "Channel that love into an area of your life that is lacking love."

What? This momentarily confused me until the Spirit guided my thoughts to forgiveness.

Remember the fairy tale I began with? Apparently, I had not fully forgiven the boy I had so deeply loved and been so deeply hurt by. I was humbled immediately as I recognized what I needed to do once and for all. Finally, and for the first time, it felt easy. Natural. Desirable. Of course I could forgive him! How could I hold back when I was feeling this much love? I couldn't hold on to the anger anymore. I forgave him in that moment. I felt a tangible burden lift off my shoulders, releasing my heart of unseen tension that had been lurking in the shadows of pain. Charity is a superpower. With the love of my Savior coursing through every fiber of my being, I was able to do something I was simply incapable of doing before and on my own.

"And charity suffereth long, and is kind, and envieth not, and is not puffed up, seeketh not her own, is not easily provoked, thinketh no evil, and rejoiceth not in iniquity but rejoiceth in the truth, beareth all things, believeth all things, hopeth all things, endureth all things."[34]

Charity never faileth. Did you hear that? It *never* faileth. So when my heart and soul feel weary, I remember what they need to be successful with a 100-percent guarantee to love as the Savior did and feel His pure joy.

I have been blessed with sweet opportunities to love and give with all my heart and find the joy in it. The Nauvoo Pageant is one opportunity. It has given me the chance to return to my mission and once more be called to serve. My heart explodes each night with the love I feel for those in the

---

34 Moroni 7:45.

audience and those I am serving and performing with. I am grateful to be able to share this love through stories of faith, hope, and healing, in both song and word. I get to spend six weeks serving, teaching, learning, and rejoicing in truth and in the people who have come to Nauvoo who need to feel close to their Savior and be reminded of the power of His love. Is this not pure joy?

I know there are many who endure far greater trials than I will ever know. I know to some, it may seem silly that I ache in the ways I do. And yet, it is because of this that I have chosen to love and use my talents as another outlet for my heart. No matter the cause, every person we meet has a heart that knows joy and sorrow. The details are not as important, but how we lift and learn together is.

"Thee lift me, and I'll lift thee, and we'll ascend together."[35]

I have experienced both sides of this Scottish coin. I have come closer to my Savior as I try to live as He did—with love. I feel I understand a bit more of how and why He was willing to offer the ultimate sacrifice for us through His infinite Atonement. Love for His Father and for His brothers and sisters not only motivated His choice to fulfill His mission, but I believe that love gave the Savior the strength and power to do so.

So, with charity pumping in every direction from my heart, I find strength beyond my own. No surprise there! For this is what we have been promised. How can I choose anything other than joy when that is the natural fruit of actively loving and allowing God to send His love to and through me.

I am thirty-one. I am a member of The Church of Jesus Christ of Latter-day Saints. I am single. I am an actress. And I am joyful.

I have boundless opportunities to share my heart onstage, on-screen, and with beautiful humans I interact with daily. Each time my heart aches, I am grateful. I am grateful for a heart that feels emotions deeply, that yearns to give in immense magnitudes. I am grateful for the Spirit who reminds my heart that sometimes it is the small and simple that will produce the greatest fruits.

What is on the current page of my fairytale?

I met a nice boy. That is all so far, and that is enough. In a recent music video, I played a woman waiting for her love to return to her. No acting needed there. It was sweet to feel even a portion of that joy I so look forward

---

35 Scottish proverb.

to. I closed a play in which I played a woman whose heart was aching for a lost son. I shared my whole heart every night.

I am going to Ghana with HEFY to build an orphanage for children who have been abandoned because of their disabilities. My heart can hardly handle the anticipation of so many for whom it will expand to embrace.

I sat next to a woman on a long bus ride who felt broken. I know, sister. I still have shards of pain lodged in the tiniest nooks of my heart. We shared our hearts and rejoiced in this shared experience of learning to love and heal.

This is my life today. This is the mission I am serving currently. Who knows what tomorrow will bring. Ah, the sting and the thrill of the unknown! The unknown might cause frustration, but it is also fuel for adventure! Which princes will gallop across my path? Which directors will cast me in the Oscar-worthy roles? With Heavenly Father at my side, I know I will have the strength to endure and enjoy every moment that prepares me for these dreams that drive me.

So I choose to live my "happily ever after" now and look forward with great anticipation to each page of the story of Kristen Leigh Metzger, a leading lady-in-waiting. Bring on the dragons. I'll fight them with great joy.

This is the Church and kingdom of God on earth. Truth has been restored. Live with confidence, optimism, faith, and devotion. Be serious about life's challenges but not frightened or discouraged by them. Feel the joy of the Saints in the latter days—never crippling anxiety or destructive despair.

—Jeffrey R. Holland[36]

---

36 "The Greatest of All Dispensations," *Ensign*, July 2007. Originally from a CES fireside address given on September 12, 2004.

Letter to Readers

I AM NOT SURE IF you have just finished reading the entire collection of stories or if you skipped to the back of the book. No matter. I just hope you know that I appreciate you. I am inspired to keep writing because of you. I read your letters and know that you are doing your best to choose joy and live a life with God.

I have a pile of letters called "For the One." I share about one in particular—Rebecca, from England—in this book. She felt isolated, and her faith was being hijacked. But as she read of the women in *I Can Do Hard Things with God*, she started to realize that she wasn't forgotten or alone.

There are Rebeccas all over the world—from Alabama to Zimbabwe—brothers and sisters who wonder if God has forgotten them or if they even have a place in His Church. I pray that readers will feel a real connection in my books. Because together, we are stronger.

Thank you to the thousands of you who have given books to people who are struggling with their own hard things, trying to forgive, and still *choosing joy*—no matter what. I believe in the power of telling our stories. When we do, we are all strengthened! It is a symbiotic relationship between storyteller and listener. And for that, I will continue.

With love and gratitude,
Ganel-Lyn Condie

About the Author

GANEL-LYN KNOWS ANYTHING IS POSSIBLE with God. She is a popular motivational speaker—known for inspiring others with her unique honesty, authenticity, and spirit. She is dedicated to her family, faith, and inspiring others. As a graduate from Arizona State University with a BS in elementary education and psychology, she became an award-winning journalist and was editor of *Wasatch Woman* magazine. Ganel-Lyn has interviewed well-known public figures, including Cokie Roberts and Richard Paul Evans, and has a talent for sharing other people's stories. She is the mother of two miracle children and loves growing older with her supportive husband, Rob. Ganel-Lyn lives with an open heart and feels passionate about sharing principles that will empower others to live life with more joy. She is a regular television and radio guest. Her YouTube channel, talks, and books have now encouraged thousands of people all over the world. Ganel-Lyn's faith and family have helped her overcome and learn from a major chronic illness and other challenging aspects of life. You can learn more about Ganel-Lyn at her website www.ganellyn.com.